Children of Bethlehem:
Innocents in the Storm

What some readers have thought of 'Children of Bethlehem'

'Behind the headlines—and the stereotypes—are ordinary people, young and old, Israeli and Palestinian, struggling to achieve a better life for themselves, their families and their country. This book tells some of their stories—admittedly mostly of young Palestinians, since the author's experience as a teacher at Bethlehem University is limited to them—stories of suffering, courage, violence and hope. They show us human faces and give us insight into the hopes and fears in human hearts.'

His Excellence Cardinal John O'Connor, New York

'This book speaks from the heart. It is a personal testimony, based on what Patrick White himself has seen and experienced as a teacher in the University of Bethlehem. I hope that his sympathetic understanding of the Palestinian people will communicate itself to all who read the book, because only in this way can there be any solution of the conflict in which they are involved. If there is a bias here, as Patrick White himself says, it is towards those who suffer: there is no propaganda in these pages.'

John Wilkins, Editor, *The Tablet*

'I hope this collection, written by a man who dedicated himself with many others to the service of man in the Holy Land, will help towards building the peace that the Holy Land needs today.'

+ Michel Sabbah, Latin Patriarch of Jerusalem

'A memorable and moving account. It is a measure of Patrick White's honesty and integrity that he allows us to see the larger picture and to entertain the hope that in time both people will be able to share their land in peace.'

Professor Maurice Harmon, University College Dublin

'This is an inside story of young Palestinians' fight and plight sensitively narrated by their foreign teacher, with some perceptive glimpses of Israelis in all our complexity and ambivalence. The writer's love and sympathy are contagious, and so is his faith that peace and mutual understanding are not only an imperative necessity but also a real possibility.'

Tamar Pelleg Sryck, Israeli Civil Rights Lawyer

'This is a first hand account of the first few months of the Intifada, movingly written by a neutral observer who happened to be on the scene. The careful description of events from day to day makes this book a rare document that will be read long after the events it chronicles have ended.'

Hisham Sharabi, Editor, *Journal of Palestinian Studies*

'There is no more troubled place in the world today than the Middle East. Bethlehem has been one of the epicenters of the trouble, despite its being the birthplace of the Prince of Peace. Brother Patrick White gives a moving personal account of what it is like to live there as a faculty member of Bethlehem University. This is a book well worth reading.'

Theodore M Hesburgh, CSC
President Emeritus, University of Notre Dame, Indiana

Children of Bethlehem:
Innocents in the Storm

Patrick White

Gracewing
Leominster

Gracewing.

Fowler Wright Books
2 Southern Avenue
Leominster
Herefordshire HR6 0QF

First published 1989
This edition first published 1992
Reprinted in 1992
Gracewing Books are distributed

In New Zealand by:
Catholic Supplies Ltd.
80 Adelaide Rd
Wellington
New Zealand

In Australia by:
Charles Paine Pty
8 Ferris Street
North Paramatta
NSW 2151 Australia

In Canada by:
Novalis
PO Box 990
Outremont H2V 457
Canada

In U.S.A. by:
Morehouse Publishing
P.O. Box 1321
Harrisburg PA 17105
U. S. A.

ISBN 0 85244 198 3

Typesetting by Kingston Press Inc. New Jersey
and Print Origination (NW) Limited Formby, Liverpool L37 8EG
Printed and bound by Dotesios Limited,Trowbridge, Wilts BA14 8RN

CONTENTS

DEDICATION

These stories are dedicated to the young Palestinians with whom I have taught, lived and learnt much.

ACKNOWLEDGEMENTS

I would first like to express my thanks to my community in Bethlehem University for their help and advice and in particular to Brother Andrew Winka, FSC, Ph.D. for his patience in introducing me to the secrets of the word processor. To Claudet Ashley, from the Old City of Jerusalem, who typed the initial text under difficult conditions.

I would also like to record my great gratitude to Monsignor Robert L. Stern, Secretary General of the Catholic Near East Welfare Association, without whose backing this project would not have got off the ground. To Brother Austin David, FSC, Ph.D, Assistant to the Secretary General of CNEWA, for supervising the editing, publishing and marketing of the book in New York and to Kristen Crowe, Administrative Assistant in CNEWA, for typing the final manuscript.

Such were the difficulties of communication from the West Bank during the Intifada that I enlisted the help and expertise of my family in London. My thanks to my youngest brother Timothy White, Director of Spots Films and to my brother in law, Doctor Anthony Pickup and my sister Bridget Pickup.

I would also wish to thank Maurice Harman, Professor of Anglo-Irish Literature of University College Dublin, for his encouragement and advice for the inclusion in the text of his poem entitled "Check Point."

And finally to John Wilkins, Editor of The Tablet in London, for the inclusion of articles written for The Tablet of the last two years and for his comment, "Why don't you write a book?"

INTRODUCTION

I've decided to write a book. Why not? Other people have accomplished the task! So I am sitting down at my desk where my window faces across Bethlehem. Below, occasionally traffic rumbles along Manger Road. Each evening the moon develops towards its full roundness associated with the autumn equinox. The darkness is filled with scattered lights and further away in the desert small Arab villages display dim pockets of light and beyond them to the South-East, brighter glares of light mark the Jewish settlements on the West Bank. Now below an Israeli jeep roars along Manger Road with its siren blaring. Yes. I'm writing this during the Intifada. The uprising is now in its fifteenth month. Last night shooting and stone-throwing, the inevitable arrival of ambulances, marked the continuation of the uprising just below our residence.

Why should I have the audacity to write about the Intifada? Hundreds of journalists are well on their way to producing hundreds of books. I'm a relatively new arrival here from England, having taught in Bethlehem University for three years commencing in September 1985. I have to admit how little I know of the land and the people with such a long complex history. I have to admit, quite obviously, I do not belong to the culture. This is a land of unpredictability too! Who could claim eighteen months ago that the Intifada would start. Who could foresee during the Intifada that King Hussein would withdraw his connection with the West Bank?

Further still, my qualifications to write a book are questionable. I can be accused of knowing only one side of the story. To think about this land there are surely rules to remember, one of which is not to choose sides. How to resist this temptation? There are very human people on both the Israeli and Palestinian sides. Both sides are capable of good and great evil. Surely too, I should face the fact the people will brainwash me. Even handedness is not common here. I should be aware also of the danger of using the easy analogy. The West Bank and Gaza are not just like South Africa or just like Northern Ireland. So too the story keeps changing; people change their positions. One should listen, listen to all kinds of views on every side. There are all kinds of viewpoints.

I write knowing that I am breaking the rules, knowing that my story is a particular point of view and that I have listened to Palestinians and have not, in this polarized situation of hatred and fear, listened to Israelis. I do realize that there is another part of the truth and another point of view. Yet I have taught and listened to the young Palestinians whom I have really had the privilege to meet. These young people, all they have known is a military occupation for twenty-one years of a most demeaning and humiliating kind, and, although I will be accused of bias, I have to accept it. In my search for human faces behind the problems of this land, I discovered wonderful human beings whom I have grown fond of and who have given me much in return.

So this short book is about my experience of meeting and teaching these people before and during the Intifada. I would like to share too the thrill of teaching them in Bethlehem University. Perhaps, also, I can dispel some of the false ideas about life in a University in the West Bank, but to be honest about the frustrations and difficulties encountered. And also to describe, in my role as a teacher, friend and in charge of Campus Concerns, my experiences illustrating the story with events, faces and personalities in the places around Bethlehem during the Intifada. I cannot claim to have much knowledge of politics, but I do not claim to be detached from the situation. As a rather ordinary person I hope, without sounding too pompous or judgmental, to be against all violence, injustice and evil and desire Peace, Justice and Goodness.

Every story is about life lived. Every story calls for question-raising, attention-holding, and calls forth a judgement from both listeners, readers and writers. Every story is informational and intends to be transformational, retaining the past so as to be aware now of the intention to do something about the future in the context of hope. This is an admonition for the situation here. Avoid despair and hopelessness and have faith in the future.

I hope one day there will be a lasting Peace with Justice. Both Israelis and Palestinians have suffered. Both peoples are suspicious, defensive, manipulative, resentful and the basis for this is fear. Fear often is psychological, but fear nonetheless. I would like to think that I have organized my stories around a conclusion and that inspite of my view of the truth in the end I can say with equal conviction, "Shalom" and "Marhaba."

I / SUNDAY LUNCH AT BEIT SAHOUR AND OTHER THINGS

It was Sunday and we left the University property shortly before midday. We were invited to lunch with Palestinian friends in Beit Sahour. It would be good to see friends, to socialize, to have a change, any variation in our lives was eagerly anticipated. The Intifada had raged for over eleven months and our University, where we worked, had been closed for over a year.

The road runs steeply down from near Manger Square to Beit Sahour. Bethlehem overlooks the town of Beit Sahour, which is located partly on the steep slopes east of Bethlehem and plateau near and around Shepherds' Field. The road straightens out, a few shops appear at an intersection and then it narrows with school buildings on one side. As we approached this area we noticed people coming out of their houses, standing on their roofs or verandas or walking towards the area with anxious faces.

"James," I said, "Let's get out of here!" "OK. I'll take you back, if you are frightened," he replied. For me it was not so much a matter of being frightened but of being prudent. We had heard before we left rumours about demonstrations and a young man shot dead. The scene was ugly and explosive when we arrived. On one side of a stone wall built across the road was a furious crowd of people of all ages both male and female. This was the angry reaction of the inhabitants to the killing of Iyad Abu Saada, a young Greek Catholic after Mass earlier that morning. The troops had rushed to the scene. Several jeeps and then a truck arrived. The soldiers were no more than twenty yards away from the column of angry people. Rocks were hurled back and forth. I saw a soldier rush to one of the jeeps returning with an armful of tear gas canisters. A medic in a white coat was attending to a figure on the ground and gesticulating to a soldier. A car in front reversed rapidly blocking the view and threatening to crash into us. We swung round and decided to return to Bethlehem and telephone our friends to see if there was any possibility of getting to them and having lunch.

Voices on the end of the line were tense. "No, don't come!" and yet in the same breath, "we've prepared lovely Arabic food, it is cooked, what a pity you cannot come!" Shortly after this, a curfew was imposed for four days. All 9000 people were confined to their homes. For us, discretion was the better part of valour. That Sunday morning in a demonstration after the Mass at the Greek Catholic Church, Iyad Abu Saada was shot by a plastic bullet in the stomach. He ran, after being hit, jumped over a wall and fell, some say, hitting his head. A doctor I know, who examined the body, was surprised that he died from such an injury. It was not clear whether massive internal bleeding or something else was the cause of death. Young men spirited his body away before the troops could get it. Four or five other people suffered gun shot wounds. The mother of the family we were about to visit, told me afterwards, she had hoped we could get through so as to take the wounded to hospital. She told me they put four of them in her car and she drove them to hospital. At the checkpoints, so as to appear casual, she played music on a tape and used her not inconsiderable personality and femininess, to persuade the soldiers she was driving the young men home.

The army, having imposed a curfew, started house to house searches all day attempting to recover the body. From what I was told, a group of young men spent the day driving a car with Iyad's body in it from house to house. They even drove out into the desert near the Herodian and hid the body in the Bedouin villages. Later, because of the heat and the rapid development of odours from the body, they drove through a back way into Jerusalem to Maqased Hospital to make use of the facilities there for storing the body. They were unable to do so because the hospital authorities said they would have to register the death and almost immediately the Israelis would arrive and take the dead young man. Meanwhile, whilst the searches continued the Mayor of Beit Sahour negotiated with the military governor in order to have a Christian burial. It was late in the evening when agreement was finally reached. The funeral took place but only a small number of mourners allowed. To the exasperation of the troops the funeral started with the coffin coming from the home of the Iyad where they had searched for his body at the beginning of the curfew.

After four days of curfew, the customary visits to the grave yard, prayers in the church and the sharing of condolences with the family in their home, were attempted. Women in the graveyard were teargased and dispersed. Those that went to the church were also driven out by the soldiers. One week after a death of Iyad, as is the Arab custom, men and women visited the bereaved family. Troops arrived firing eight canisters of teargas into the home. Three of the men were in such distress they were taken to the hospital. That Sunday was also marked by a religious procession. The Greek Catholic Patriarch Bishop Lutfi headed the peaceful march. Troops attempted to disperse it but the Greek Catholic leader persuaded the Military Governor to allow it to proceed.

The death of Iyad and those injured in the Beit Sahour incident were overshadowed in the press by the appalling petrol bomb incident in Jericho, where an Israeli mother and her children perished in the flames. Palestinians I know, were dismayed by this awful action. They wondered who was responsible for it and felt it could not have happened at a more sensitive time, just before the Israeli elections. I was talking to one of the local Arab Mayors and I asked him if he had any hope as a result of the forthcoming elections. "Forget it," he snapped. Perhaps he was being realistic.

Now that the results are known of both the Israeli and American elections, I can feel an atmosphere of depression and sadness among the people in Bethlehem.

Before the elections we saw an intensification of the measures to control the uprising. The University had been closed for almost an entire year from October 1987. During October 1988 the closure, was intensified, I was leaving the Brothers' residence, which was on the University property to see if I had any letters in my postbox in the administration offices. As I entered the area I met a bright, pleasant young man, who had a doctorate in mathematics and who lectures at the University . He came from a large Christian family in Beit Sahour. I breezily greeted him with: "Kif id-dinya l-yom? koies?" [How's your world today? Good?"] (Throughout the text the English equivalent for these Arabic phonetics will appear in brackets) I was slow to see something was wrong. "I just want to get home!" he replied, with uncharacteristic tension. I then looked out of the window and saw several jeeps and troops blocking the main gate.

Apparently at around 10:30 A.M., two jeeps parked outside the main gate of the University. A Major Mufid insisted on seeing the Vice-Chancellor and demanded he collect all the personnel on the campus. The Vice-Chancellor answered that the safety and freedom of personnel could not be jeapordized, and said he required a written warrant. Minutes later the Military Governor, Colonel Lavic arrived, allegedly with a warrant from Jerusalem. Brother Anton de Roeper judged it best to allow Colonel Lavic, with a limited bodyguard, into the campus. He discovered only administrative staff. Some identity cards were taken and later returned. Later on the full rigours of military closure were applied. Only the resident Brothers and some of the Sisters plus essential maintenance staff would be allowed on the property. A list was prepared for approval.

Meanwhile the uprising has virtually become a way of life. Now we rarely go to our windows when we hear the almost daily shooting. Yesterday, however, I saw a squad of soldiers rushing after some young teenagers, firing at them as they gave chase after a demonstration in which they were throwing stones at the soldiers. It seemed somehow quite ludicrous to me to observe highly trained troops of one of the most powerful armies of the world in hot pursuit of a group of what appeared to be twelve, thirteen and fourteen year olds The tragedy of all this is all to apparent when I see a twelve year old boy at the handicapped centre, with his leg amputated, a result of a high velocity bullet.

What follows is the explaination of how I came to be driving our battered brown Renault down the untidy road to Beit Sahour on a Sunday morning at the end of October 1988. It is the story of a bystander living and working in Bethlehem for over three years. It is the story of how I lived among Palestinians, before and during the uprising.

II / I ARRIVE

It was dark when we left Ben Gurion Airport in 1985 to drive up the now very familiar road to Jerusalem. September evenings in the Holy Land were warm compared to the cool windy day at Gatwick Airport. I had experienced my first rigorous security check before boarding the charter flight. I had arrived and was on my way to Bethlehem to serve on the staff of the University there.

It's always difficult trying to explain who I am and what I'm about. I belong to an international group of men who devote themselves to Christian education. We are known as Christian Brothers and often as De La Salle Brothers in Ireland, the United Kingdom, Australia and the Far East, after the name of our French founder who lived three centuries ago in France. In the Catholic Church we would be categorized as a lay service religious congregation. Lay, in this case, means we are not priests but Brothers. That is, we live in communities where we direct our energies towards education, especially of the young who are underprivileged or have particular needs, caused by economic poverty or because of a lack of justice or peace. Our life leaves us free to be of service. We are free because we are not married with family commitments; we are free because we make ourselves available for service; we are free because we individually do not own goods or property.

I arrived with two cases of mainly clothes. I did leave behind a wind-surfer and a tea chest of notes, books and odds and ends. I bought some warm clothes, because instructions from the University advised adequate layers of clothing, for in winter at 3,000 feet it gets chilly.

Where was I coming from? I was for six years headmaster of a Christian Brothers school on the Island of Jersey. They were six fruitful years, directing the development of a school which had a long tradition in the Island. I believed, at that time, that six years was enough. Each institution, particularly an educational one, requires new ideas and leadership. Nevertheless it was a painful parting in many ways but a correct one. I was asked to apply for interview for the head of department of Geography at St. Anselm's School in Basildon. I found it very hard to go for interview when only a few days previously, as headmaster, I interviewed new staff for Jersey: good for the soul perhaps!

Anyway, I joined a school which had one of the best staffs I had encountered in my years in education. There was a strong sense of devotedness, community and professionalism. I also wanted to experience life in a Comprehensive school. The cultural shock was considerable. Although I think I managed, I was hardly satisfied with my performance and felt that these vibrant young people needed a younger teacher who understood their needs better than I. My time, at St. Anselm's, also coincided with the teacher's pay disputes, the cuts in education budgets and the general fall in morale that accompanied these developments.

Life in one's middle forties often offers opportunities for change. I started teaching in 1960 and apart from two very happy years off doing a second degree at Queen Mary College London University and four months on a Human Development Program at Sante Fe College, in the United States, I taught, coached, housemastered and headmastered for twenty-five years. The suggestion that I apply for a teaching post in our University in Bethlehem came as a providential one. I applied and the Vice-Chancellor offered a position in the English Department.

So here I was leaving Jerusalem on the road through its suburbs of Talpiot towards the West Bank. The lights of Gilo, a new Israeli suburb of Jerusalem, built on Arab land, shone as from some vast limestone fortress. Gilo, in fact, is made up of high density appartments. We passed by the Tantur Institute, an ecumenical centre I was to visit on a number of occasions. In the dark a few fields with olive trees, scattered Arab houses and then Bethlehem Rachel's Tomb, the roundabout and the winding route of Manger Road which gradually circles the high ground with its dimly lit streets which eventually led us to the community residence. I discovered our home was situated under some Palestinian shops, a series of small simple rooms with a linking corridor. The Brothers were all there to greet me: six Americans, one Czeck, one Palestinian and James, the Englishman who met me at the airport. My room had a bed, a simple cupboard—" closet" I was told by the Americans—a desk and a chair. There was a small window that looked towards Beit Sahour. The walls were simple concrete with plaster and yellow paint. The view from the window was blocked by a Palestinian home which had apparently only just added another floor. People retire to bed early in Bethlehem. I was ready after the journey to get some sleep. I noticed I had company in my room, a gecko and a rather large one at that. He became my friend and companion for the next few months, a pleasant obliging fellow who kept insects and mosquitoes at bay. And so I slept.

I was awakened by what sounded like a very loud buzzing noise. Half dazed, half asleep my mind raced to discover where I was. An unfamiliar bed, a room with early morning light beginning to stream into the dark encompassing space. The noise? Then suddenly the realization that I was in Bethlehem and Muslims have mosques and mosques have gentlemen—i was later to find out called Muezzin—who pray through loudspeakers and apparently set the volume for sound quite high. This particular establishment sounded really close to the house. I got up and looked out. The sun was coming up over the limestone desert hills from Jordan. I could see the mountains of Moab shrouded in the morning haze and the white clusters of buildings stacked up against the hills of Bethlehem. Yes, I had arrived. This was a new beginning.

III / BEGINNINGS

The walk up to the University is a pleasant one at 7:30 A.M. in spite of its position on the highest hill in Bethlehem. From Manger Road there are a series of steps leading first to Star Street and when a short walk through this narrow street is achieved, another set of steps up a passageway past houses and stone walls to Frères Street. It's a good morning constitutional and in the days that followed an opportunity to meet the local people who are so friendly.

"Marhaba!" [Hello] was the first word I learnt. I found out one can say this to everybody. It's expected; this is the Palestinian welcome and friendship. I couldn't imagine myself walking down Bromley High Street in South London at 7:30 in the morning and hailing all I met with "Hello!" "How are you today?" But in Palestine: "Marhaba!" I said: "Marhabten" replied the old Arab man as he struggled down the steps, "Kif Halak!" [How are you] I queried "Hamdella" [Very well] he replied "Shu ismak?" [What's your name] he asked "Ismi Patrick" [I am called Patrick] I answered. Arabic is a difficult language to learn and I still struggle to learn the basic greetings and conversation.

Mixed feelings, if I recall, were my response to the arrival at the main gate of the University. High walls, large panelled steel gates prevented any view of the inside for the person arriving. Was this a prison, perhaps? I had a lot to learn about living under occupation. The small campus of 17,000 square metres leased from the De La Salle Brothers back in 1973 was surrounded by high walls and on top of these, tall steel railings. The gatekeeper wanted to see my I.D. I had not got one yet and after some persuasion, I slipped in through the small steel door.

So this was it. Back in 1972 under the auspices of the Vatican a committee was set up to examine the possibility of establishing a place of higher learning which would offer a broad education in Arts and Sciences for all Palestinians in the West Bank and Gaza, but particularly for those in the East Jerusalem and Bethlehem geographical area. The property had been used for a high school run by the De La Salle Brothers, who have conducted Schools in Turkey, Lebanon, Jordan, Egypt and Palestine for over one hundred years. Apparently some eighty students registered in the first year in the new University, utilizing the existing school buildings. As I entered I noticed a small courtyard and the old main building with its clock tower and statue of the child Jesus on the top. Attractive and quite spacious gardens with paths and trees on two terraces faced out across Bethlehem towards Beit Sahour, providing a fine view and a shaded area where dozens of students sat quietly chatting to each other. I discovered later that the lower terrace was known as "lover's walk." New buildings housing the Science faculty, a fine modern library and a large multi-purpose structure, still under construction, indicated the growth of the institution. The enrollment at Bethlehem University numbers 1597 students 1425 of whom were full-time. So really Bethlehem University was a small liberal arts college run on the American college administrative design, management, academic organization and curriculum.

Beginning, would mean acquainting oneself with the American ways of doing things. At the first English Department meeting, I think there were over twenty of us. I heard such phrases as credit hours, semesters, G.P.A.s, unit tests, quizzes, majors, minors, electives, honors, grades and so on. I think the system is highly organized, and it did take a certain amount time to adjust, particularly the grading or marking as we would call it in United Kingdom. In the American system 70% is a passmark. In England 70% is a high score and 50% the norm for passing. Maybe my marking was considered too low at first. Yet with the team teaching in the Intensive English Programme and the painstaking marking done with scripts graded by several teachers, the standards soon became apparent.

During the first week before lessons commenced there were all the activities associated with beginning the autumn semester. Faculty meetings were a novel experience. The Arts Faculty met for a brief meeting. The dean's English was none too good, so I had my first experience of Arabic in a rather rhetorical style. The English Department gathered in the boardroom, and if I recall we were about 50 percent native speakers. Brother James was the chairperson. Business was friendly and orderly with minutes taken. The expatriate staff were for the most part, like myself, religious from a variety of congregations. The full faculty meeting gathered in large science lecture hall. Brother Thomas Scanlan, a six-foot-three New Yorker with a powerful administrative mind gave a formidable address. I also became acquainted with all the vice-presidents, a very American idea, Executive Vice-President, Financial Vice-President, Academic Vice-President and Development Vice-President and the Deans of Arts, Science, Nursing, Education and Business.

Late in the afternoons I would walk with James across the karstic desert hills surrounding Bethlehem. During the hot siesta period these two English men would take 6-10 mile trips visiting neighboring villages, Solomon's Pools, the

Shepherds' Field, walking as far as the Herodian and back in the heat. We would practise our Arabic with friendly villagers. Time and again Palestinian villagers, we had never met before, would insist we stay for tea or Arabic coffee. "Ahlan, ahlan" [Welcome, Welcome], they cried. On most occasions we made polite excuses saying we were "mashi, mashi," our phrase for going for a walk. James' fame often went before him. If graduates or students of his, saw him coming there was no escape. Dazzling oriental beauties and smiling young men would greet us demanding we meet their families. Tea with mint was a most refreshing drink in the heat, with fruit and coffee following. After coffee, we were allowed to leave. I soon began to discover the friendliness of these people and I think they drew out from me friendship in return. I recall later doing the Myers-Briggs test in Seattle University. Earlier before the Bethlehem University experience, I found my extrovert-introvert scale, (or preferences), was mildly extrovert. Last year in Seattle, I found my preferences wildly extrovert. I really do put this down to the wonderful friendliness of the people and our students particularly.

And so life for me in Bethlehem started and continued in this simple style. We were up with the early morning sun. Whilst the Muezzin's voice, filled the air with the "God is great" we recited our daily office and prayers. When the semester finally started, classes commenced at eight and ran through to four or five. By early evening we were back in our cellar-like apartment under the shops along Manger Road. Each evening we seemed to disappear underground, hibernating as it were, for the cold nights to pass and to prepare for the next day. Gradually the heat of summer began to fade and the nights became mercifully cooler. Mosquitoes too declined in numbers and annoyance. My gecko was there to meet me when I returned to my simple room. I had borrowed a small radio that was stored in one of the cupboards. People at home in the United Kingdom will never realize how encouraging it is to listen to the B.B.C. world service, especially to hear the objective news and on Saturday afternoons to Paddy Feeny with coverage of the football and other sporting events.

In spite of the evident hardship of our simple home, the sometimes obvious isolation of living in a different culture, the growing awareness of the injustices of the occupation and the strong aspirations of the people, I was happy to be in Bethlehem. It gave me the newness and challenge I required. I felt wanted and needed and useful again.

IV / THE STUDENTS

I met my first class in the lecture rooms beneath the library in late September 1985. This was section E of the Intensive English course for freshmen: twenty-two young and not so young Palestinians. A slight buzz of excitement and expectation filled the room. I began to read their names out. There was evident good humour as I made numerous mistakes in spite of practising the list beforehand. Ahmad, a tall and serious-minded young man. Ali, in his thirties and imprisoned for ten years, was desperate to make up lost time and wanted to find a wife, build a home and become qualified. And Amal, one of the eight young women students, a very serious-minded, independent Moslem young woman, clothed in the traditional long dress. So too was Bassma, a very sweet and good natured woman student from a village near Hebron.

Fusan was quite a character. He stood well over 6 foot 3 inches it seemed. He was the tallest freshman for the year, he proudly claimed. He came from the North near Tulkarem. He had a sense of humor and an element of mischief. We became friends and although his English never became very strong, for he later majored in Sociology, we always chatted when we met. During the three week strike against the administration at the end of the Autumn Semester it was Fusan who blocked my way into my classroom to prevent the lesson from beginning. Naturally this action and the strike itself puzzled and distressed me. This again was another element in the learning process. All authority, even the efficient and at times somewhat tight administration at the University, would appear a threat to oppressed young people under occupation, particularly to those students who were failing out. Two years later, during one of the demonstrations Yousef helped carry the dying Isac to the nursing department. Isac was shot in the head, Fusan's jeans were stained with blood. With water and salt we managed to work out most of the stains so as to avoid his arrest at the roadblocks. Mary, I discovered later, was married. She had a powerful character, and although I rarely made a point of consciously identifying Christians or Moslems in my mind, it became clear that her social and religious background and her personality clashed with a group in the class. Her English, especially her spoken English, gave her an advantage. Students from the private schools, especially the Christian ones, generally gained a stronger command of English than those students in the public (state) schools. This, however, was not true for many of the other disciplines.

Khaled, Khalil, Nouh and Taha all lived in the Deiheisha refugee camp. They were the first group of students to invite me to their homes. Inspite of their poverty and the dreadful conditions in the camp, their welcome and hospitality I will always remember and cherish. At the end of November, after I had made numerous excuses for not going to their homes, I was escorted through Bethlehem to the area near the Square where we filled a service (taxi) and drove off to Deiheisha. I was taken from one small dwelling to another that afternoon and evening, and introduced to their families and offered food in each house. Three years later, when I visited the camp, I continue to meet them. Most of them, like many of the young men in the campus had experienced various stretches of imprisonment; Nouh had been in prison for fifteen years. I was to learn more about these experiences later; suffice it to say that their friendly personalities and genuiness captured my sympathy and affection.

Other faces of my first class came to mind. Mohammad, Naji, Jehad and Salim all struck me as most courteous people. Manal, now married, an intelligent attractive young woman; and Magdolaen, a singer was full of fun and quite extrovert; Siham, Suzan and Joanna, all quieter, younger students, nevertheless hard working. And then, My'Awiah, I could never get his name correct for a long time, he kept a low profile in class, he found English difficult. Also Mahmoud, keen, sitting at the front, while most of the men would sit further back, worked hard and constantly asked questions. Such was the first class I had contact with in the Autumn of 1985.

The student body in Bethlehem at the beginning of Autumn Semester 1987 numbered 1597, of whom 1425 were full-time and 172 part-time. Fifty-five percent of the total were male, the remainder female. The number of female students is remarkable and reflects a considerable change in the attitudes of Palestinian families towards tertiary education in a mixed environment. Girls from the villages south of Bethlehem, for example, villages generally composed entirely of Moslem people, now come to the University. Sending their daughters to receive a liberal arts education, which in many ways was so different to the pattern of social mores and codes in their villages, was really remarkable. Obviously this dichotomy did not exist without its strains on the students. The girls sometimes found their roles in the University clashing with expectations at home. Here they could sit and talk freely with men. Occasionally they fell in love or were friendly with Christian young men. Generally I felt the experience and opportunities to receive a university education for the Palestinian women one of the great contributions made by the University.

So too was the interaction between Christian and Moslem students on the campus. At the beginning of the Autumn Semester 1987, sixty-seven percent of the students were Moslems and the thirty-three percent Christian. On the West Bank only six percent of the population is Christian, so thirty-three percent of the student population at Bethlehem University is a commendable number. I found generally the Christian and Moslems mixed well and enjoyed life together as students. Both Christians and Moslems had extensive friendships with each other. However, I became increasingly aware of the fears of the Christian community at large in the Bethlehem area of encroaching Moslem power and control.

In my own experience I found I became closer to young Moslems in the day-to-day interaction on campus. I was not conscious of this, until some Christian students complained to me. This was not a choice on my part, for in so many cases I did not register at all students' religious background, but really enjoyed them in their full humanness and goodness. Possibly too, someone from the West, who was somewhat disillusioned with manifestations of our culture and affected by them, found the wonderful human qualities of young people from the rural areas particularly attractive. Also many of the students, both Christian and Moslem, from the large centres, such as East Jerusalem, were to some extent westernized. There can be no doubt in my mind that the University, apart from its specific academic contribution, has made an equally important impact on Christian-Moslem relationships. It has led to a more liberating role for Palestinian women, and I hope, enhanced the human and spiritual values of all those involved.

Geographical distributions - part of my training was as a geographer, so I cannot overlook this - of the student population also added additional perspectives. About thirty-four percent of the total come from the Bethlehem area, which includes students from Beit Sahour, Beit Jala and Deiheisha Camp. Beit Sahour is a strongly Christian village, generally composed of tightly knit families who are middle-class and often highly educated. Many of our staff come from this village. It also has a strongly independent and politically aware population, often very highly qualified academically and professionally. Many of the Christians are Greek Orthodox, though there are Greek Catholics as well as Latin Catholics. Beit-Jala too is strongly Christian, with an increasing population of Moslems. Both areas have strong individual identities. Bethlehem is no longer a predominantly Christian centre. Nearly thirty percent of our students come from among the Palestinian population of East Jerusalem and its surrounding satellite villages. A good number of Christians and Moslems reside in the old city. Again some of these are associated with the service or commercial activities of the region of which tourism is an important segment.

From the Hebron region come eighteen percent, all Moslems, many from agricultural backrounds. About seven percent come from the north in Ramallah, where there is a Christian enclave. Approximately another three percent of the students still further north are Moslems who live in camps, villages and towns as far north as Nablus, Tulkarem, and Jenin. Not included in the figures are a number of students from the camps and towns of the Gaza Strip. Approximately five percent of our students currently live there.

So the great bulk of students reside within reasonable distance of the University. Those from Hebron do not travel so far, but the length of their journey depends on where their villages were located. Students from the north or Gaza rent rooms with families generally in Bethlehem. The girls' hostel quite near the University can accommodate only 40 students.

Gradually I became more aware of the stresses students were under because of the occupation. The generation of young people I taught were totally imbued with the effects of the Israeli occupation. For most of them, the twenty- one years of military occupation was all they remembered of their wider life experiences. I recall earlier in my teaching chatting with students in one of the courtyards in the sun. In the course of the conversation I pointed to someone across the yard. One of the students quite emphatically asked me not to point, for it made individuals nervous. Gradually I came to know how insecure many were. On the campus the Israeli military would have their informers gathering intelligence about students and staff, and particularly what the Student Senate was up to. The Student Senate was predominantly a political body, elected each year. The various clubs or societies — such as the football club — were only really a name. The various political factions of the PLO such as Fateh, Popular Front for the Liberation of Palestine (PFLP), Democratic Front for the Liberation of Palestine (DFLP), the communists and the Moslem brothers all competed to gain control. This of course was another pressure on the individual students, many of whom, though good Palestinians, did not want to be involved in the web of politics, and who wanted to concentrate on their studies.

Although intellectually I understood that it was only within the universities and the camps that Palestinians had any chance to express their aspirations, I did not always accept this emotionally. One of the deepest frustrations was to face interruptions, some of them really quite uncalled for, by the Student Senate. With the experience of the Intifada and the appalling treatment imposed on the Palestinians, particularly the young, I can understand more fully the students' attitude. I will say more about this later.

For the occupying military, the intelligence branch is vital. How often at 7:30 in the morning, having finished our prayers—we were now living on campus—we would be surrounded by troops. The yellow Mercedes bus remained stationary in its parking space, indicating that the driver could not get in. Arbitrary road blocks would prevent the University from functioning. The military might have had information I certainly did not have, nor in most instances, I am quite sure, did the administration. The information must have its source and more than likely within the student body. A number of students told me how they would be called to the military and asked to inform. Often the secret police, the Shin Bet, had ways of putting pressure on the young people. In some cases the students' brothers were in prison. Prison sentences, especially if a number of years were involved, could be lightened with assistance and cooperation. Bribes, promise of future employment, quicker permission to go abroad were other possibilities. Drugs, money, easily available sex, too, pandered to the weaknesses of some. One year it was obvious to the administration that the elected senate contained an informer. It was only after the graduation of this individual that members of the Senate believed this. The young man was warned not to come anywhere near the University. Back in October 1987, however he did come near the University, apparently just outside the main gates in a small coffee shop. I was serenely teaching Tennyson's "The Lady of Shalott" in a classroom not more than 50 yards from the gate. Out of the corner of my eye I saw three or four students with kaffiyeh hiding their identity, and later followed by an anxious Dean of Science, pacing their way across the outer courtyard. In the middle of discussing the possible romantic characteristics of "The Lady of Shalott", shots rang out. I've never seen twenty-five students get through one door so quickly! Apparently, the four disguised students had left the campus, leaving the Dean of Science at the gate, and entered the cafe, beating up the informer with clubs. As the students retreated into the property, the gates were open, I think to let a car in or out, another car drew up outside the cafe, a revolver was given to the bleeding young man, who wildly shot six rounds in the direction of the fleeing students. From what I can gather the young graduate informer has disappeared.

I met in Rome a Sacred Heart Father from South Africa, who was completing his doctorate on the techniques used by the South African administration to control and infiltrate the black student bodies. He told me that many of the techniques originated from the French attempts of suppression in Algeria in the late forties and fifties. I told him how students, after a demonstration at Bethlehem University, were arrested when it was fairly clear that they were no way involved. Detention often lasted more than eighteen days. When they returned they were often viewed with suspicion by the student body. Had they, during their long detention, become informers? Techniques to spread rumour, suspicion, mistrust are part of the continuous pressures put on students by the military occupation.

When there was tension I began to identify this during class time, especially the first 8:00 o'clock classes. Students arrived late, some, particularly the girls, upset by the treatment received at road blocks. It was not infrequent that the men had their I.D.'s taken. This meant reporting to the Military Headquarters in their area, where humiliating and demeaning treatment took place. Also, if students knew a demonstration within the University was due to take place, it was very difficult for them to concentrate. Events in Lebanon, American bombing raids in Libya, commemoration of the horrors of Sabra and Shatilla and particularly Balfour Day caused unrest.

I now look back at the last three years of teaching to see how remarkable the young Palestinians were. They, inspite of all the pressures on them, particularly those from the camps who experienced frequent curfews and harass-ment, remained cheerful, humorous, friendly and to a great extent diligent in their studies. Some obviously were more damaged than others or had taken up politics at the obvious expense of their studies. These to my knowledge were only very few.

V / TEACHING

The English Department at Bethlehem University runs a number of service courses, one of which is called Business Communication Skills, designed specifically for the Business Faculty. In my second year in the first semester, I was appointed to teach three of these classes. One of the practical experiences the students encountered involved telephone skills. Generally the students in the department were bright, but their standard of English varied considerably. Those who were fluent at school found the course easy, whereas students who had a weak background and of necessity followed Intensive English Courses in their first year, lost much of their English by their third year, as most of the teaching and classwork they were exposed to was in Arabic. Part of the exercise in the practical use of the telephone involved preparing a description in English of hypothetical business. Some chose printers, others car sale distribution business and so on. Members of staff from the English Faculty kindly volunteered to acquaint themselves with a particular student's hypothetical business. Using the University's internal telephone system and my "campus concerns office", specific staff would phone up their student. In one case the member of staff, who actually owned a Fiat car was attempting to buy a new one. He met his match because the student's English was perfect and, unknown to me, he worked part-time in his father's Fiat Dealers' Centre. The student came to me rather amused. "He owns a Fiat and knows nothing about it! Furthermore, he is trying to buy a new model that doesn't exist!"

Other students were less fortunate. One, whose English was not strong, made out that he was the manager of a hotel in Beit Sahour. The member of staff, a most meticulous and precise customer, claimed he was in Jerusalem and wanted to stay in the hotel. After the usual enquiries, that the manager struggled to answer, the customer asked for directions by road from Jerusalem to Beit Sahour. This threw the student, who in exasperation broke out in Arabic "Shu Hada". [What's this]

And continuing, approximating the troubled Arabic, "For heaven's sake, the hotel doesn't exist. Why would there be a hotel in Beit Sahour after all! Why are you so bothered about how to get there." I can sympathise. Try speaking on the telephone in a foreign language for the first time.

The classroom setting is very simple. In the old buildings we now have false ceilings, so voices do not echo. In spring, summer and early autumn, the classrooms are naturally warm and the windows are open. In winter however, it can be cold, wet and at this altitude occasionally very cold with strong winds. The students sit huddled in coats, kaffiyehs around their heads, sometimes breathing steam from their mouths in the freezing atmosphere. There is no central heating. The floors are flagstones or tiles. There is a blackboard and chairs with a writing surface attached. In these circumstances, the teacher tries hard to use limited resources to best advantage and I must say that my teaching methodology has improved. Back in England I used overhead projectors, audio visual equipment, slides and displayed material especially when I was teaching sixth form Geography and Economics. Having a first class honors degree in Geography, I thought I was quite confident that I knew a little about what I was saying and frequently fell into the trap of lecturing. In Bethlehem, the American system backed by an excellent Teacher Development Office, encouraged everyone to teach and not to lecture. This was done at the teacher's invitation, with videoed lessons, in order to assess the teacher's performance in a non- threatening way.

I also appreciated the flexibility with which chairs without tables could be arranged in groups, circles etc, to facilitate the different student activities during a lesson. Most of my lessons in English, whether literature or language, were broken up into seven segments or activities with a minimum of lecturing and maximum of student participation. Lesson preparation for this type of teaching requires a great deal of time. Worksheets, handouts could be prepared, typed and printed because there was more time available in a University setting. Marking in English is a heavy task, particularly in writing courses where English majors follow advanced communication courses in their second year. American textbooks on essay writing and rhetoric took the student through the rigours of writing logical and well structured essays. Unity, topic sentences, coherence, controlling ideas were all concepts the writing of English required of young people who had a different way of thinking, a different way of arranging their ideas, a different and most beautiful form of writing that goes across the page from right to left, the reverse of our western style.

A random walk round the University during class time would reveal lessons punctually started—full attendance was much stricter than I had experienced when at university—diligence and serious involvement on the part of the students. In nearly every case, though there were obviously exceptions, motivation was high, attention easily held and rarely were there occasions to use authority or to impose discipline. The young people were, I found, polite and courteous, and classes were held in an atmosphere of good humour and pleasant purposefulness. In fact the Palestinian students were really a delight to teach.

Many English undergraduates had a natural feel for the rhythms and flow of poetry. By the third and fourth year they could enjoy Shakespeare and Donne. Maybe they would miss some of the subtleties of language and humour in "As You Like It"; but so too do native speakers! The best students are as good, I'm sure, as anywhere. One young man, Jamal, confined to his wheel chair, read fifteen of Shakespeare's plays for his English Seminar in his fourth year, drawing together a masterful thesis on the role of clowns entitled "Men of wisdom in camouflage." The seminars were great festivals, where the whole fourth year would attend and a large number of the staff came to listen to the oral presentations and to ask questions. Students would dress especially for the occasion and sometimes friends and family would attend.

I think it is true to say that when Palestinians enter the University as undergraduates they have certain approaches to study that are cultural, but also the result of the Jordanian secondary school examination system. Their fondness for learning by heart is immediately apparent. Maybe this approach is derived partly from the rote learning of their religious texts, especially by the Moslems, who revere their Koran as fixed and indisputable. I think too, the methodology used, much of it memory work again, in preparation for the Tawjihi examination at the age of 16-17 years of age, is a contributive factor. Also there is a tendency to accept the written text, because it is written, as final. Further still, there is a tendency to give equal weight of importance to every part of the text. Status too, plays a vital part in their society. The teacher in the classroom is unchallenged. The higher the status of the speaker, the more worthy of attention he/she is held. Also Palestinians tend to express communal rather than personal opinions. This is reflected strongly in the Student Senate where its decisions often go unchallenged. So it is a challenge in class for them to think for themselves. Mind you, I do not consider the failure to make them think is an uncommon one. Look at the English system! But here I'm talking about a fairly extreme situation. It is a rewarding experience to educate them to think, analyse, evaluate, synthesize the material set before them. Class discussions eventually become second nature, the teacher, once infallible, becomes an animator who is challenged too.

I recall now, with the experience of hindsight, my mistakes, quite dramatic at the time, in returning grades or marks to the students. Sixth-form teaching in England, which I enjoyed immensely, was a cosy friendly affair. Essays were set and marked, sometimes discussed without undue excitement or rancour. The American system at Bethlehem involves a series of unit tests, numerous quizzes, a mid-semester evaluation and a final examination. Maybe it is partly this complex system imposed on the students; maybe it is part of the Arab culture. Whatever, I can assure you discretion is needed in the manner of giving back "marks". My first unit test in my first Intensive English class I returned within the first ten minutes during the first lesson of the day. The papers were distributed in a classroom electric with apprehension. Almost immediately excited individuals came to explain that surely their grade was too low.

"Why is this wrong?"

"Jehad has the same expression and he got more marks!"

It was like a forest fire, nervousness fanning the flames. For the freshmen anyway, I was later advised to adopt certain procedures. One cynical old-timer made the following suggestions. I return the papers during the last lesson of the week and at the last second, and then beat a hasty retreat for the weekend out into the Judean Desert. Actually more humane methods existed for both student and teacher. Also, as the students matured and gained in confidence and became accustomed to the system, their reactions became more controlled. Nevertheless it came as a shock even though I had been warned. Furthermore, though frequent tests are probably the best method to make sure the work is done, I hardly find their complexity and frequency really educational.

Arab learning too has a tendency for imitation rather than creation. Essay writing, particularly creative writing, often reflects the ideas from the texts or from what the teacher has suggested. Originality does develop, however, but it takes time. When it does there is much richness to enjoy. As Allan Bloom in his "The Closing of the American Mind" witnessed the decline in reading during his time as a teacher in American Universities, so too I've noticed how our library at Bethlehem is under utilised. Many students love to sit out in the gardens; in the lovely sunny weather under the brilliant blue skies and in the shade of the trees. They have their texts, they discuss and talk with their friends, but most reading of associated material is left to the very keen. Also very few of them have elaborate files. Their notes, references, worksheets are tucked into their textbooks. I've always wondered how they find specific information, but it seems to work.

Gradually I became aware of the pressures that existed for many of the students, particularly those from the refugee camps. We had a considerable number, over a hundred from Deiheisha and a smaller group from Aida and Azza camps, all of them in the Bethlehem area and quite close to the University. Students also came from camps near Ramallah, the Gaza Strip, between Hebron and Bethlehem and I believe from Jericho. They were subject to constant harassment from the military. Young men, with grins on their faces, would arrive late for eight o'clock class.

"A little trouble", was all they said. Perhaps it had become an everyday experience for them. Deiheisha was under curfew. They managed to get through the cordon of troops via the hill at the back, or sleep out at friends' houses. Nor did they tell you that all the males from the age of 14 up had to sit cross-legged on the school playground all night, and this punishment occurred in the cold wet winter.

A student would quietly tell you that his papers and books had been destroyed. He would be studying at night, the troops would break into the house and order all the lights to be turned out taking his books at the same time. It took sometime, to be able to ascertain the genuiness of some excuses for work not completed. There were authentic cases of students who were being followed by the Shin Bet—the secret police—or the soldiers, and who went from house to house to escape arrest. During the semester students would disappear and not been seen again. They had been arrested and were in administrative detention for eighteen days or several months. This was the experience of students not just from the camps but from all over the West Bank. Roadblocks were a frequent problem to face for those travelling to the University. Buses loaded with students were stopped and all of them lined up. Their books and papers searched. Palestinian literature, even Palestinian flags drawn on their books or notes could well result in the confiscation of their identification cards or even their arrest.

Loss of an identification card meant the individual was obliged to report to the military. Humiliating and demeaning treatment followed. Students that returned from imprisonment were most reticent to tell of their experiences and when I first listened to some of them I did not believe them. Later, when I asked a Red Cross official whether there was any substance in the students' reports, I was left in no doubt that much of what I was told was basically true.

Looking back at my three-years' experience I am not at all surprised at the present Intifada that now rages on the West Bank and Gaza Strip. I am amazed at the standard of work achieved at Bethlehem, considering the pressures and constraints of occupation. I wonder, with sadness, what academic life will be like once we are able to resume work after the Intifada. I fear how the appalling policies of the Israelis are breaking every element of human rights with regard to education, forbidding any teacher to teach any child in any place at any level of either primary and secondary. Head teachers from the Bethlehem Schools were assembled and lectured by the Military Governor, who, left them in no doubt about the consequences of teaching even one child in a private house. The implications of nearly a year without continuous education for the children of school age is hard to quantify. The damage done to the individual child, to the schools and to the quality of candidates for higher education, such as entering Bethlehem University, must be considerable. I think in terms of just the quality of those who wish to become English majors. While the schools were open, so I am told, the quality of English teaching had declined in some of the schools, something we noticed and in order to cope with this the Intensive English Program was designed.

It seems a long time ago that we enjoyed the activity of the classroom with the students. For me there can be few occupations that can compare with teaching when it is going well, and, both teacher and students are enjoying the experience. It seems a long time ago too, that we would venture into Jerusalem with students for cultural events organized by the British Council or some other agency. I recall, with amusement, a musical evening sponsored by the British Council held at the Frères School which is located just inside New Gate, and adjoining the wall of the old city. It turned out to be a rather heavy jazz concert. On to the stage walked six English ladies attired in what can only be described as a "women's lib appearance." Once they were settled down amidst a mass of cables, wires, amplifiers and other such impressive electronic equipment, they proceeded to produce a great deal of noise for about two hours. Let us say it was all rather different, or at least a new experience, for the Palestinians. There were only about 70 in the audience in a hall that could comfortably seat 250. One could not help noticing as the proceedings reached a terrific intensity with the six young ladies caught up in various postures of pain or screaming ecstasy, groping shadows of dazed Palestinians, their faces unusually pale as the lights flashed on them momentarily, were struggling for the door and the peace and solitude of the walls of Jerusalem.

This perhaps was not one of the most cultural experiences. I remember later trying to have a short walk on the ramparts. Three armed Israeli soldiers stopped me and said the walls were closed. It was a feast day.

"I have set watchment upon your walls, Jerusalem, which shall never hold their peace day or night." (Isaiah 62.6)

VI / HAPPY DAYS TALKING AND WALKING

I am looking back to what had been, before the closure of Bethlehem University twelve months ago. The memory of life before the closure and before the Intifada remains in my mind. Memories can be selective, the subconscious cutting out the unpleasant experiences, hardships and suffering. My feelings, for the two years from September 1985 to October 1987, still evince a sense of well being and contentment. We did have pressures, maddening interruptions, military closures but they did not last long. Most of the time was spent constructively, teaching and caring for the young men and women attending the University. The teaching was a real joy and went well. Also, I shared many other experiences with the students and staff in our day-to-day interaction, in the work of the Campus Concerns Office and the limited range of other extra-curricular activities on and off the campus.

I was appointed to be in charge of "Campus Concerns" at the end of 1985. I was loath to lose any teaching and mentioned this to the administration. It seemed to me that classroom, if one enjoyed it and did reasonably well, was an excellent starting platform for pastoral work. Also, the Campus Concerns Office was very much in its infancy, and was furthermore a western concept, which did not readily fit with the Arab mentality. So I dropped only one class and inherited a well setup office and lounge. Students, staff and friends of mine, came to the office to congratulate me. I had a large metal desk in an office of my own — previously I was packed into one of the little rooms with three other staff on the arts corridor — to the eastern mind I now had special status. Amusingly, so I'm told, a large metal desk was the prerogative only of those staff with doctorates. Their Arab mentality picked this up immediately.

"Oh, Brother Batrick!" The Palestinian has great difficulty in pronouncing P's or in fact writing P's, just as the westerner becomes contorted attempting to utter the throat sounds expected when speaking Arabic.

"Oh, Brother Batrick! Shu Hada! [What's happening] You have done well, your office is bigger than Brother James'." (James if you recall was my boss as chairperson of the English Department).

"How is this, you are not as important as Brother James?" Again, status means so much in their lives. The ostentatious houses, the bigger, the more ornate and decorative they are, the more they reflect a person's level in society. So here I was with a large lounge and a separate office for meetings, interviews and so on.

In the United States, Campus Concerns would generally come under the umbrella pastoral care or be called campus ministry. In Britain, the nearest to my experience were the chaplaincies in our various universities. In Bethlehem, because we cared for both Moslems and Christians, Campus Concerns was the term used. When I was appointed I asked the Vice-Chancellor what his expectations were. There was a long, perhaps pregnant pause, after which he said, "Values, yes, I think values." This was a pretty broad and vague canvas with which to work! I guess there are human values with strong spiritual qualities for both Moslems and Christians. Obviously, I would like to think that I was inspired by Gospel values too. The University handbook was more specific in stating the goal as the enrichment of the University commmunity and providing counselling services and coordinating service programmes. Since the two professional counselling offices operated independently and there was a well organized and acredited community service programme for all students in their third year, I saw my role as Director as seeking to strengthen the sense of community among students, faculty and administration.

The whole concept was of course very much in its infancy and very new to both staff and students. Even some of the prominent Palestinian staff on the administration viewed the operation with suspicion.

"Why all the free coffee and tea?" they asked. It was as if the eastern mind was attempting to discover some ulterior motive. Students too, were hesitant, particularly the more politically minded, those associated closely with the Student Senate and political parties. Advice, given by experienced practitioners, counselled me not to try too hard, but to go slowly and gain peoples' confidence. I imagine I was asked to undertake the role because I enjoyed the students' company so much. Corridor talk, stair talk and garden talk or sitting around sipping Arabic coffee in the canteen were some of my occupations and were still to be, I think, an essential activity.

The concept presented a challenge to me. Although I really experienced only one year and a few weeks in the job before our closure in October 1987 and the advent of the Intifada in early December 1987, the time was a pleasant and rewarding one. In early October the freshmen all visited the office and were invited to give it a name that summed up its role in the community. The resulting competition and prize involved great fun and quite an amount of discussion in the Arabic Department. The best name was "Harbour," but its translation into Arabic presented academic and linguistic problems. We held Friday afternoon discussion groups. One of the most moving was a panel of four students describing their experiences in prison. A girl, Rima, explained how she was imprisoned with Israeli women prostitutes and drug addicts and was only moved to other accommodations when she went on a hunger strike, claiming she was a political prisoner. Another student explained how administrative detention operated, and Nouh described his fifteen years in prison. Students and staff mingled together and shared questions and ideas. These panels and discussions continued during the year. Life in refugee camps, problems of stress and pressures from the occupation were debated. The future of Palestine was also discussed. Doctor Jad spoke on self-reliance, something that did develop later during the Intifada, and for which he was arrested and imprisoned for six months. I'm quite fascinated as I look back and recall how we were shocked by some of the prophets of doom and destruction, and yet these were close impending events, closer than many of us thought. Friday afternoons became a meeting time in the Harbour. Concerns and issues were aired and I think the spirit of community enhanced.

I experienced great joy in encouraging outings. The different departments had social organizations called "families" and some excellent trips were undertaken. Because Palestinians are so restricted and have few opportunities of travelling on the coach trips, they use buses that have Israeli number plates. It would be very difficult for them to travel in Israel with Arab number plates, for they would be stopped at roadblocks and turned back. With this new freedom they travelled far north to Haifa, Banyas, Tiberias and the Golan Heights. They would leave at sun rise at 6:00 a.m. and return at 9:50 p.m. Though I enjoyed them, I felt exhausted after a day mainly in the coach seeing how far they could travel. Also the level of noise toleration for an ageing westerner was quite different from that of young exuberant students from the Middle East. Loud Palestinian songs, interspersed with excited deafening announcements over the microphone, were continuous.

I recall, however, one trip with the English Department Seniors, their last before graduation where I was the only member of staff available to go with them. Generally several staff travel too and enjoy the outing, not specifically in any supervisory role, though foreign staff are a help if the coach is stopped at an Israeli checkpoint. This particular journey took us to the beach at Natanya, a fun park and a zoo near Tel Aviv. During the stay in the park one of our students had his camera stolen. He discovered that some young Arab men from Gaza had an identical model, and he recognized it as his, but could not prove it. I had seen the group of young men from Gaza earlier. They were dressed in colorful western suits and appeared to be under the influence of alcohol or drugs. I was waiting in the coach, and I was concerned that we should be away promptly, as we needed to be back on the West Bank before dark, particularly since the women students had to travel from Bethlehem to their homes and villages. The coach suddenly emptied of men and then the women got off. Left on my own I went to investigate. Down in the park a large group of Palestinians had gathered around a hot debate taking place in the centre of a gathering of over, I should imagine, a hundred and fifty people. I became concerned when things appeared to be getting rather excited and voices and gesticulations quite dramatic. Over half an hour had elapsed since the students left the coach. I approached, in my ignorance, an Israeli policemen and through various intermediaries persuaded him to come with me. Almost, as soon as we arrived the problem resolved itself. It was an excellent example to me of the way in which Arabs settle disputes. After much debate, a reliable bus driver from Ramallah was asked to take the camera. He would take it to Ramallah that evening and have the film developed. I later discovered the film was developed and our student received his camera and photographs back. On the West Bank and Gaza many disputes are settled in this fashion without reference to law enforcement or lawyers. On the way back to Bethlehem everyone was overjoyed with the experience and revelled in the unity displayed by the student body.

I began asking students who visited the Harbour, to organize trips independently of the "families". The main reason was my urge to see them get more exercise and to enjoy walking their land. A secondary factor was the element of politics that was creeping into the various departmental "families". Political parties from the Senate wanted to control the outings. Bickering and friction resulted. Jamal was one of my great hikers and organizers. We had wonderful days walking from the Herodion to the Dead Sea across the desert, hiking down Wadi Kelt to Jericho, trips to the coast staying the whole day on the beach swimming and playing volley ball or football. On one splendid day we took a mixture of the administration, academic staff with their families, secretaries and students in local buses to the caves near the Herodion enjoying the walks down the Wadi, the desert flowers, exploring the caves, picnicking and singing. On another occasion by the sea, I remember very well, one girl student from a village near Hebron, who was clothed in the traditional Arab dress and who had never seen the sea before, sitting by the water's edge in a trance, gazing at the ocean and the rhythmic patterns of the waves.

There were local walks too. James and I walked with two students who were fifteen years together in prison. The conversation was fascinating and amazed both James and me. How could two men, who had suffered so much be so calm and even minded. A girl student from the nursing department was with us. I was curious to know why she was walking. Saleh said she was his wife. They had just married, recently. He told us that the last time he had seen her just before he left prison; she was five years old. He married her shortly after his release. At the time of this writing Saleh is now in prison again in the Negev. He is an admired man in Deiheisha who does much to help the suffering people. He was most anxious to avoid politics; it was the quality of his leadership which caught the notice of the Israelis.

Another walk I remember with nostalgia, was in my first year before I was involved in Campus Concerns. Several staff arrived at the meeting point in Manger Square. Only one student turned up. His name was Isac. He was a special friend of Sister Margaret, an American Dominican nun from the deep south near Memphis. We walked across the hills near Bethlehem and up the valley that leads to the beautiful village of Ertass where Solomon, apparently had his gardens. Today the horticulture is well ordered and watered in the valley from the reservoirs further up in Solomon's Pools. It was above in the forested area where we had our picnic by one of the large reservoirs. One of the photographs taken I made into a Christmas card. I recall two years later visiting a close friend in Jersey at Christmas — I had returned to England as my mother had died — seeing the Christmas card from the previous year hanging up to his cosy dining room. It shook me. The picture, I had forgotten all about it, was of Isac, the only student to go on that particular walk. At the end of October 1987, Isac was shot through the head in a demonstration at Bethlehem University that resulted in our closure. People in his camp, Aida Camp, will tell you that they consider his unwarranted death, a prelude to the Intifada.

There was a particular group of delightful young students that accompanied me on several walks and short bus trips. They were musically inclined and a variety of guitars and other musical instruments plus some splendid song voices came along. The singing on the yellow Mercedes University bus was wonderful. It was fun and laughter all the way. I remember, specifically going to the coast one weekend. We were travelling near an Israeli army bus full of young women soldiers. They could not see our Arab Bethlehem number plate or the University name on the side of the bus. Jeries, the lead singer and guitarist was a particularly attractive man in appearance and personality. The Israelis shouted across in Hebrew and some of our students answered in Hebrew.

"What beach are you going to? Can we join you there?"

Their attractive faces and long black hair were somehow enhanced by their neat uniforms and fetching black army hats. Their faces were pressed against their bus windows. Smiles and blowing of kisses made it all the more poignant when the inevitable happened. The car in between the rear of their coach and ours pulled out and our true identity was revealed. The row of cheerful faces turned, and all we could see were the back of their heads and stiff shoulders.

Really how sad. Two groups of fine young people, one moment enjoying each others' company only to be divided by the fears of national identities and the histories behind them.

I think it was Carl Jung, the German psychiatrist, who said that everyone longs to tell his or her story to someone and have it understood and accepted. It's my desire to say how exceptional my experience was with students and to acclaim it. Telling a story works both ways. The person who tells the story bestows a gift on the listener. And I hope those who might read this and appreciatively receive my story will bestow their gift on the teller. May your gift be one of empathy and sympathy.

VII / STORIES OF STUDENTS

I count him as a friend as well as a student of mine. I will call him Khalid, though that is not his real name. His is bright, articulate, interested in serious things, and very religious. He lives in Deiheisha Camp, is now in his early twenties, and has been in prison four times; on one occasion for seven months.

He writes stories in English. They are not entirely fictional. The one I include here really reflects his own experiences and the well documented experiences of hundreds of other Palestinians and their treatment when arrested and when in prison. He calls, his story "The Dead Olive Tree Comes to Life."

He was not asleep yet. Something from within urged him to stay awake. It was one o'clock in the morning. Nervously, he lit a cigarette and began puffing the smoke in the darkness. Suddenly, he threw the cigarette through the window and put his head on the pillow. Before he could close his eyes, several knocks were heard on the outside door awakening all the family. As soon as he heard the knocks, he jumped out of bed and went to open the door. As he stepped into the hallway, he saw his mother who signed to him to return to his room. She waited until he closed the room's door. Then she opened the door.

When the door opened, many soldiers rushed into the house and took positions in every corner of it. After that, a strange looking man, who was wearing civilian clothes walked in — he was the captain.

"Good morning," he greeted smiling, and he waited for someone to greet him back, but no one did so he continued, "Where is Khalid?"

At that moment and before anyone could reply, Khalid came out of his room wearing his clothes as if he was ready to go with them. He was 23 years old, tall, handsome with dark complexion, sharp eyes, black hair, and broad shoulders.

"I see that you are ready," the captain said sarcastically.

"What do you want," Khalid asked sharply.

"Give me your I.D. card,"

"Take it."

After the captain had taken it, he commanded the soldiers to search the house, but nothing was found.

"O.K. you will come with us now."

"I beg you not to take him. He did not do anything," the mother said, shedding tears.

Quickly, Khalid came near her and kissed her hands.

"Mother," he said, "Do not be afraid, I will return," he smiled trying to comfort her.

"Not before some years," the captain laughed.

One of the soldiers gripped him by his shoulder and pulled him out of the house. When he was out, he saw many soldiers surrounding the home—some on the roof, others in the street. Three big Jeeps stood 20 meters from the house.

Suddenly, the soldier pulled his arms behind his back and put handcuffs on him. So he could not see anything, a sack was put over his head which reeked of sweat and dust.

"They will torture me to death," he thought.

A sense of fear overwhelmed him because it was the first time for him to go through this experience of being arrested. The rotten smell from sack seemed to suffocate him. Their angry voices confused him because he could not understand what they were talking about. Then he was put in the jeep which lurched forward into the darkness carrying him to the unknown.

When they took the sack off and unlocked him, he could not tell where he was. It was a big room without furniture. Nothing but some chairs here and there. Three soldiers were looking through angry eyes at him.

"Take off your clothes," one of the soldiers shouted.

He knew from his friends that this happens to everyone who enters the jail. "They use it to humilate the person and to search him," he remembered what his friends had told him. He took his shirt off and pulled his trousers down.

"And your underwear."

His face became red. He stood still without doing anything.

"Are you shy? Take it off bastard," the soldier shouted with a loud guffaw.

"I must not show fear," he thought. Then he took off everything. He felt naked and humiliated. He fell into a violent rage, he wished he could cut them into pieces.

When they had finished searching the clothes, they threw them at Khalid who quickly put them on. Then they handcuffed him again and put the sack over his head. One of the soldiers caught him by the sack and pulled him as if he was an animal.

His shoulders struck the walls everytime he stumbled. When this happens something inside him rebelled and he wanted to kick the soldier, but he feared the results.

Suddenly, the soldier stopped and unlocked him. Then he hung his hands up and tied them to a small pipe so he could not move.

"I do not want to hear your voice. Do you understand?" The soldier shouted.

"Yes," Khalid replied.

Khalid was punched in the stomach.

"I told you that I do not want to hear your voice," the soldier laughed.

The punch was very painful. He tried to sit, but he could not. The rotten sack made the problem worse and worse; he could hardly breathe. The pain spread to every part of his body; his chest, arms, shoulders and his legs.

Five hours passed before anyone spoke to him. Nothing was heard except some painful cries coming from the nearby rooms. His legs were shaking. He could not feel them as if they were not his. The shoulders were hurting. It seemed that someone was pulling them out of his body. His neck swung from side to side.

"Did they forget me? When are they going to interrogate me," he thought. His eyes were very tired.

"I want to sleep," he shouted, but no one spoke to him. His stomach was empty. He felt sick and dizzy. He knew that he would faint and....

When he opened his eyes, he found himself sitting on a wooden chair. He was in a small room. In front of him, there was another chair beside a wooden table. In the wall, a small window protected with bars overlooked a rocky mountain. The walls were stark, but there were some terrible pictures on it; pictures of devils, and people being tortured.

He was still feeling dizzy when the door was opened. A man, wearing civilian clothes, entered. Smiling, he went near to Khalid and said, "Do you feel better now? I will punish them. I told them not to touch you. They are monsters, but you must not be afraid now; I am with you," he smiled again.

"What do you want from me?"

"You must know that we have all the information about you. For example, you had your lunch in the "Happiness Restaurant" two days ago. Then you went to visit your friend, Ahmad," he smiled," you stayed there for two hours. Correct or not ?" he asked.

A deep depression gripped Khalid. He was very confused. His heart beated fast.

"How could they know this ?" he thought, then he looked at the investigator and "Why did you arrest me?" he asked firmly.

"You ask me! It is you must answer this question."

"I do not know why."

"It is no use to deny anything, you are an educated young man. Your cooperation will keep you above water."

"I do not know what you are talking about?" Khalid shouted. The investigator opened the door and looked back at Khalid who was feeling his shoulders.

"I will see you tomorrow. I hope that you will cooperate with me," he said and went out closing the door behind him. A few minutes later, the door opened and four soldiers streamed into the room and went directly to Khalid. They looked him up and down. Without saying a word, they began beating him all over; his face, stomach, chest, back, legs, and his head.

Khalid was trying to transform the torture and pain into resistance and challenge. They did not stop until they were tired out. Then they dragged him out of the room to a prison cell.

It was a dirty cell full of strong offensive smells. The air was full of moisture. The coarse walls were greenish. A disgusting smell submerged the cell. There was no water, no food and no window. Nothing but ragged blankets. A bitter silence overwhelmed all.

Khalid was very exhausted so he collapsed on the blankets. Then he began examining his face. It was pale and pinched and very painful; his mouth was bleeding his eyes were swollen and his nose was broken.

He lay back trying to sleep. "Are they going to torture me again," he thought. Many questions were going in his mind. "Is my mother crying? Who will help them and work to raise the kids? Are they going to destroy the house?" His eyes filled with tears. He tried to shed tears, but he could not, so he closed his eyes and quickly he fell asleep.

After he had slept for three or four hours, he opened his eyes and tried to remember what had happened to him. He was very hungry and half sick. His body cried for water. He had to eat and drink so that he could bear the awful torture. He stood tottering and knocked the door with his fist.

"What do you want, you dog," someone shouted. Khalid was filled with anger.

"I want water and something to eat," he replied angrily.

"You want to eat! After five minutes you'll have a good meal."

Khalid reclined on the blankets. The five minutes seemed to be five days. He suffered the tortures of hunger, thirst and pain. The door was opened and the soldier appeared.

"Get out," the soldier shouted.

"Where to?"

"To have the meal of course, where else?" the soldier laughed.

Khalid stepped out of the cell. Another soldier came and put the sack over Khalid's head besides handcuffing him. Then he was pulled until they reached the investigator's office. The sack was pulled off. The handcuffs were unlocked. The investigator came in.

"How are you?" he asked.

"I am hungry, I want something to eat."

"You did not eat!" he said in mockery "I see that you have been tortured," he continued. "They did not give you food. Yet they torture you? Those monsters," he shouted." I told you, they are savages. Cooperate with me and I will deliver you from this hell. Do not be obstinate."

"What do you want from me?" Khalid cried.

"Who hung the flag in the last demonstration, in your camp?"

"How could I know?"

"We know it was you. Why do not you save yourself the torture?"

"I did not do anything," he shouted.

"You are stupid, they will kill you."

"I did not do it, I didn't do it" Khalid repeated it many times.

"I will go now. When you are ready to admit; tell them to bring you to me."

Then he shot out of the room, slamming the door behind him. Suddenly, five soldiers entered the room. They grabbed him by his shoulders and took him to another room.

They tied his hands to the ceiling. A cold quiver ran through his body. Merciless, they began beating him; they used clubs to hit him on the ribs. Khalid shouted from pain. He felt as if he was dreaming; living a nightmare. He could not believe it was real. He began to hear the sounds and voices as if they were coming from far away. Everything was rolling before him. The screams turned into deep groans then nothing. He passed out.

They untied him so he fell roughly to the ground. One of the soldiers brought a jug of water and splashed the water on his face.

In slow motion, he opened his eyes and looked at them strangely as if he did not know what had happened or as if he was trying to remember that. This did not last long, but soon he was dragged to another room.

He was forced to sit on a chair. Then they tied him with a rope to the chair. A stove was brought and put very close to him. He screamed and moaned painfully. He begged them, but they did not care as if their hearts were drained of mercy. He was screaming and they were laughing. He was suffering and they were enjoying it. He was begging them and they were spitting at him. His face became red. He was sweltering.

They untied and stripped him. He was taken to a small room. It was very small; just about his size so he could not move. As soon as the door was closed, cold water spilled from a small pipe in the ceiling.

He felt that his head was going to explode and his bowels were torn into pieces. He screamed as if he was out of his mind. he was kept in that terrible situation until he lost consciousness.

It took him a while, when he opened his eyes, to know that he was in the investigator's office. He couldn't move his body. He seemed to be a mass of pain. He suffered a terrible headache. He suffered from colic. One of his ribs was broken. He could hardly breathe. His eyes were half opened. Through a fog, he saw the investigator standing at his left side.

"What do you say now after you had a simple meal," the investigator said smiling.

"I... I... I will tell you... everything," Khalid said in a weak voice.

"Good, good. You are clever. Here is a paper and a pen. Write everything you did."

Khalid took the pen in a trembling hands and wrote:

"I, the under signed, Khalid Salim."

Unwillingly, he turned his face toward the window and caught a glimpse of a dead olive tree. Then he continued writing:

"I confess and admit that," once again he looked towards the window and seemed to see green branches coming out from the dead olive tree.

Smiling, he stood and tore the paper. Filled with confidence, he turned his back on the investigator.

◆   ◆

The second story is biographical. It includes in it many of the experiences of so many Palestinian young men. What is to be remembered about Nouh Salameh is the severity of his experience and his mature response to it.

Nouh is now happily married to Rehab and they have a six month old baby boy, Ibrahim. My years at Bethlehem University coincided with his. He was the Nouh I met in my first Intensive English class in 1985. It was in May 1985 that he was released from prison after spending fifteen years in captivity. Nouh was part of that much publicised exchange of, I think, over a thousand Palestinian prisoners for the release of a small number of Israeli soldiers in Syrian captivity.

His home was situated on the lower Eastern slopes of Beit Jala. From his veranda the busy Hebron Road traffic could be seen and heard across the valley that separates them. On the Hebron Road stood the faceless, utilitarian, architecture of a British Mandate fort, now occupied by the Israeli military command for the Bethlehem area. The slopes of both sides of the valley had that semi-rural flavour. Scattered houses, many of them relatively new, and some indeed quite palaces compared to the poverty of Deiheisha Camp further South, nestled near the fields of squat, sturdy, olive trees.

My friendship with this rather extraordinary man has continued over the years. Often I have sought his advice, gone on journeys to villages and camps with him. He is, after all, a local hero, admired and liked by his fellow Palestinians. It is as if for one half of his life, he lost all his freedom and now enjoys a freedom of speech and forth-rightness which at times are quite challenging. His wife Rehab is a caring and perceptive woman, who is on the staff of the local hospital in Bethlehem. Both of their parents came from the village called Zakariya which used to stand near Beit Shamesh. Their families were involved in the tragic events of 1948. When I asked Nouh where he came from he quite emphatically said "Zakariya." But I said, "you were born in Deiheisha in 1952!" This is a trait of most refugees. They tell you where their families were before the refugee movement, even if they had not, in fact, lived in the area themselves.

Nouh recalls their family of four boys and six sisters living in a tent until 1959, first at Al-Arroop Camp, and then in Deiheisha. He said their village exodus from Zakariya in 1948 was brought about by fear. The villages around them were taken by the Israelis. Rumour of killing and rape caused the people to panic and flee into the hills near Hebron to a village called Haras. His father treasured the ownership of two cows. A cow cost 50 Jordanian Dinars, a year's earnings; eventually one was stolen.

I asked him about his childhood and how he felt. He said it was not a happy one. The tents were exposed on the hillsides to the cold winter weather. Trenches were cut around them to drain off the heavy rainfall in winter. There was never enough food. He did not see or eat fish until he was fifteen. There were no oranges on the West Bank and at first very little fruit. His mother kept chickens and on feastdays, once or twice a year, these provided meat. There was no work, nowhere really to play, and life centred around the confines of the camp. He said Deiheisha was considerably bigger then, than it is today. After 1967, many refugees moved into Jordan. The UNRWA education services, he said were excellent. In fairly limited conditions, schooling was of a high standard with good teaching, which was additionally attractive, because there were no distractions. Most refugees received a good elementary, and a good secondary education.

The year, 1967 was pivotal in his life. At the age of fifteen he realized that crushing defeat of the Arab armies during the six-day war and the consequent Israeli occupation meant that Palestinians would have to liberate themselves. In 1967 he became involved in politics. With his classroom friend Saleh Abu Laban he started writing, by hand only, political pamphlets. By 1968 the fierce resistance of the Palestinians in Jordan at the village of Al-Karameh against the trained Israeli army gave him further confidence of the need for the Palestinians to free themselves from the occupation. "This battle," he said "was very important to our revolution." He told me he was the first with Saleh to put up Palestinian flags in Bethlehem in 1968. We exchanged knowing looks, both visualizing the multiplicity of Palestinian flags that appear each day during the Intifada. Later, Nouh and Saleh stole a typewriter from the UNRWA school to facilitate their writing. During this time he was imprisoned twice but only for a week in each instance.

"The struggle," he said, "deepened." By 1970 he received some grenades from Gaza. These were used at night against Israeli troops. Four months later, friends of his were involved in a clash with Israeli troops in Gaza. Some were killed and others injured. The injured, under pressure, implicated Nouh and Saleh with the use of weapons. Both were arrested and sentenced to eighteen years imprisonment. They were seventeen years old.

I asked him how he felt about this part of his life, looking back now, as he is essentially a man of non-violence, and seeks peace. He said he was young and at the time there seemed no way without violence. He said, "In 1970 no one would help the Palestinian people." He mentioned that Golda Meir declared there were "No Palestinian People." Sadly, violence has a long and pervasive presence in this part of the world.

"How did he face the prison sentence?" I asked. "How did you feel?" Prisons back in 1970 were apparently worse than the present places. He lived in a cell with fifteen others, four metres square, with just a bucket for toilet facilities, four blankets provided for under and over the body; there were no mattresses for the floor. Food consisted of half an egg for breakfast, a watery soup for lunch and a small evening meal. There were no books, plays or reading material for the first two years. Later a chess set was allowed for two hours each day. They were exercised twice a day for half an hour on each occasion. Clothes were any size, and could not be changed. There were showers, though the water was limited so often they returned with soap on their bodies. Every prisoner had to address the police, or prison officers as "Siddi" [My Master], which implies the prisoner is a slave. Possession of a pencil or pen, not addressing the staff correctly, resulted in beatings, isolation cells and no visits from families for two months. Prisoners were disciplined, when walking around the prison, they had to move with their heads bowed and their hands behind their backs.

Nouh said he did not despair, his friendship with Saleh continued. They talked and listened to each other. They would pace their prison cell for hours sharing and listening to each other's suffering. They did not give up hope. As the years went by, and they were moved from prison to prison, eight places in total, they heard of various U.N. initiatives and efforts by leaders to resolve the Palestinian problem. Prison became a way of life. They were determined to keep their sanity. They exercised, did press-ups and eventually were allowed to read. In the Beir-Sheba prison, between 1974 and 1976. Nouh was in charge of the library. He read voraciously especially in the political and socio-economic areas. Literature too, was a favourite, the

Russian novelists pleased him most. Bernard Shaw became his top English author. This commitment to reading, exercise and companionship, he said, saved him from the mental illnesses, depression and health problems that affected many of the long term prisoners.

I asked Nouh whether prison changed him. "Yes," he said. Although in many cases the Israeli staff in the prisons were harsh, he did meet good, thoughtful, men. Slowly his attitudes to them changed. He felt that many Israelis were unaware of what was really happening on the West Bank. He became conscious of their problems, their fears and mentality. He could not countenance a solution which did not include a state of Israel. He saw that hatred was not an answer. There must be a solution for both peoples.

"You learn to be in captivity," he remarked. "You begin to understand others more. You have all the time in the world to watch human nature, you search for other peoples' motives, you study human nature. You begin to distinguish between good and bad the genuine and the false."

Nouh and Saleh were released in May 1985, three years before their prison term officially ended. Life for them was strange. There were big celebrations in Deiheisha for several days. It took them a long time to adapt to a very different pattern of life. Life had changed, their families had changed, they had changed. They were used, for example, to getting up with the sun and living a strict orderly life. They found their families did not share this. Television was trivial and uninteresting for someone who had immersed himself in Dante, Shakespeare, Descartes, Marx and Tolstoy for nearly fifteen years. But prison was not a waste, as far as Nouh was concerned. He had suffered for the Palestinian people. Though many of his contemporaries were married, often highly qualified and had left the camp, he felt respected, had more freedom to speak without fear and the ability to build his life anew.

This freedom to think, consider wisely and courageously was often manifest in the time I spent with him in Bethlehem University. If he had a problem or disagreed with you, he would tell you. If the problem was big, in true Arab tradition, he would go to the top. Father Michel Sabbah, the President of the University would occasionally visit us from Amman. Nouh would do battle with the secretaries to see him. "He's my president as well as yours," he declared. Now the Latin Patriarch of Jerusalem, Father Sabbah, a native Palestinian, happened to be passing through the office at this moment. Father Michel, in his unobtrusive way, called him and Nouh had his chat. In an environment where the mistrust resulting from the occupation and indeed from the characteristics of the culture. Nouh's honesty was remarkable.

At the time of writing, during the Intifada he is distressed that his close life-long friend is in prison. He feels bad about Saleh's arrest. "He was only doing good," Nouh sighed. "He can't say no to anyone. Maybe, if I was living in the camp, I would be arrested too! People think I'm still in politics, I'm not, I think of persons!" There was pain on his face, as though he felt torn between his clear understanding and his emotions. I felt for him and sympathised with his dilemma.

I received a letter when I was away in Seattle, during the summer of the Intifada, from Nouh.

My Brother Patrick,

Thank you for your card, we are safe until now. My wife and my baby send you their best wishes. We are looking forward to seeing you in our country again. Pray for us and for our people. Please send our message to the American people. We are not terrorists. We are human beings. We love peace. We don't hate the Jews.

Your friend,

Nouh

This short letter, written in an unsteady hand contained, for me, a powerful message. Here was a Moslem quietly spelling out what it meant to be a Christian. Here was a very human person, who had suffered and lost his youth in prison, praying for love and peace, without rancour or bitterness. Here too was a man of no great religious practice, but full of wisdom, and the spirit, telling me who I was. In my struggles through Vatican II and my mid-life I had almost lost my identity and belief in my role. A Moslem from Deiheisha camp told me about my brotherhood to men.

Wise men came from the East.

VIII / POLITICS OF PROTEST

It was after a demonstration. The campus was littered with debris, the acrid smell of tear gas, now invisible, still hung in the air. During the lull, while the administration negotiated with the military outside and the Student Senate within the campus, one student thrust a tear gas canister in front of my face. "Read this" he said. Printed on the side of the canister, which was still warm, I read it was "Manufactured in Pittsburgh, Pennsylvania, U.S.A."

"Are you an American?" he demanded.

"No" I said "I'm British, from England, London."

"So you know about Balfour, the English are responsible for this mess, and the Americans continue it," he looked at me with hard eyes. I realised by now, the significance of the Balfour Declaration of 1917 when, from the point of view of the Palestinians, they were betrayed by the British, and the promise made to the Jews of a homeland in Palestine was the cause of the present injustice. I did not know the student and decided the best thing to do was to listen.

He spoke with an analogy which reminded me of a similar approach I had read somewhere. "Suppose," he said firmly, "the English lost a war and were occupied by the enemy, say the Germans." I tried to imagine this. After all I was a war baby born in 1939 so I had (vivid) memories of evacuations in 1944 and V.E. day in 1945.

"Suppose your enemy, now that you are defeated, took all of the best land in S.E. England and invited another people, let's say from Africa, to live there. The English were driven out by fear and violence up into the hills of northern England, where they lived in camps, they became refugees." By now a small group of students had gathered round.

And he continued. "And suppose the English revolted against this injustice and fought these new people again. They lose because the new people from Africa are supported by a powerful country outside. The new people now occupy all of England and try to crush the English culture and traditions and way of life. These new people from Africa want all of England! How would you feel?" he queried. I had to admit that, although it was a hypothetical example, I would not feel too good, in fact I would be very angry.

The analogy was apparent and cleverly chosen. From my reading, Palestine, it would appear, was inhabited by Palestinians. In fact in 1917, when the British were losing the 1st World War and sought American involvement, partly through the powerful Jewish lobby in USA, the Balfour Declaration was formulated. At that time nine tenths of the population were Arabs, who lived in harmony with the small Jewish community.

Another student in the group eagerly intervened. "If I have a house, and people come and take half if by force; this is bad. But then they send their children into the half that remains to us, we must fight to get the whole house back. It is all or nothing!" Such was the exchange, or rather my listening to the feelings of those students that afternoon in November. The group left. The main gates were opened and hundreds of students filtered out having experienced another demonstration. That evening, and the next day, arrests would be made and twenty or so men would be imprisoned.

It became apparent to me, only after a short while, that the universities were, apart from perhaps the refugee camps, the only places where the Palestinians could express their aspirations clearly and occasionally demonstrate against the very real injustices they felt. The administration, teaching staff and students faced the complex and often difficult roles of furthering a rigorous academic programme and at the same time coping and living with the political protest that needed expressing. Now Bethlehem University is completely sealed up. At the time of writing, only the Brothers, who live in community on the property may enter, while the Intifada rages all around us. Now I can understand, what at the time appeared to be very frustrating and often unnecessary political manifestations on the part of the students, particularly from a small core of politically orientated young people. I can also guess, because obviously I do not really know, as it is a well kept secret, where many of the leaders of the Intifada come from. They are the academically trained, the thinkers, who over the past ten to fifteen years, have passed through the universities.

The Student Senate at Bethlehem University is undoubtedly a powerful and influential organization. Each year in spring the various political parties canvas votes for seats on the Student Senate. There are elections which really are fascinating, since it is the only occasion these young people have to express their freedom to vote. The structure of the Senate involves two powerful positions, the Presidency and the secretary's position. There are clubs too. These clubs nominally are responsible for social, sporting and other activities but in reality they just provide seats on the Senate for the rival political parties. The Student Senate would occupy much of the Dean of Students' time as well as the Executive Vice- President's attention. Demands made by the students on the administration were continuous. It became particularly difficult for the administration when the Senate was divided within itself. Decisions and agreements made, were later broken because one faction, for a variety of reasons, refused to comply. It was remarkable how well, over the fourteen years, Bethlehem University functioned with both academic semesters and a summer school completed each year. Every day lost by closure from the military, from a student demonstration or political gathering would be "made up." Work would continue on Saturdays and the semesters extended.

Undoubtedly the Senate was a very necessary organization to channel the political aspiration of the young Palestinians. Politics is often an unpleasant business and quite naturally there was a fair number of undesirable elements within the University. The great majority of students were not actively engaged with the parties. At election time considerable pressure was exerted on all students to vote. Occasionally there was unnecessary and unfair pressure, and in some cases a form of bribery. One girl told me that the members of one party threatened to tell her parents she was having a relationship with a boy in the University that her family would not approve of, unless she voted for them. On the darker side too, those elected to the Senate were not always the leaders; these would work behind the scenes or even from outside the University. Looking in my notes of December 1985, I recall how a very successful semester, almost completed, was spoiled by a students' strike against the administration. Thirty disconnected and random demands were made, the crucial element involving the lowering of academic standards. The strike lasted over the Christmas period, and examinations and classes were delayed until the end of January, in order to complete the autumn semester. At the time the whole thing really seemed so counter- productive and frustrating for most of the student body. Some of the individual demands could have been made and discussed and accepted without a strike. Unfortunately a number of influential students were failing out and wanted either standards lowered or a delay. I found the whole experience most taxing and draining, particularly as the students stayed on campus with a sit-in that lasted over two weeks.

Gradually I perceived how an oppressed people feel, mistrust all authority, and will adopt extreme and often uncompromising positions. Though I experienced several stoppages by the students for political meetings during class time that were caused by students who had examinations and wanted them delayed, there were also genuine political meetings responding to everyday events. Back in November 1985 the Tunisian Affair caused road blocks preventing the students from coming to school. The Senate, however, when we were able to get to class, would have its meeting. Perhaps two hundred students would attend, as each political party speaker made an impassioned speech in Arabic rhetoric. I recall attending midday Mass in the large University chapel, and hardly being able to follow the prayers as amplified speeches reached a deafening crescendo from the cinema-hall close by.

As I look back now I think I can trace a gradual worsening of the situation, a greater tension on the campus and an uncharacteristic pessimism creeping into the students' lives. Back in September and October 1986 the killing and injuring of students at Beir Zeit University and its subsequent closure for four months increased the unrest on the West Bank. All the staff and student body at Bethlehem University stood in silence for a time on the courtyard that day. The following day we were severely road blocked. The troops would not let in some of the Brothers, who had either been buying bread early at the Salesians' bakery or collecting relatives at the airport.

The increased pressures manifested themselves in the Senate. The faction of the PLO that followed George Habash often disagreed with Fatah which supported Yassir Arafat. It became even more difficult to settle problems between the Senate and the administration. Furthermore, a growing group of the Moslem Brotherhood began to wield a considerable influence. The regeneration of the Islamic movement, already apparent in Gaza and other areas, was taking hold within the University. The Palestinian Christians feared this uncompromising movement. Demands were made for a mosque on campus: this delicate situation was not new. The expatriate Christians had great sympathy with the spiritual welfare of so many fervent praying Moslems. The Vice-Chancellor, nevertheless, had to consider the Christians of the Palestinian Churches and the implications of a mosque built on the property, and point out to the brotherhood that he could not accede to their request.

The Senate, therefore, had a strong influence on the life of the University. One aim of the occupying power was to crush the political and cultural aspirations, hopes and history of the population. The Senate would organize and encourage cultural occasions. The students' Cultural Fair was an event organized by the Senate. In the evenings, dances, songs with performers in traditional colourful dress were arranged. Several times troops tried to stop these celebrations, which were occasions of rejoicing. I remember the very professional Bir Zeit dance group unable to get away late one evening. Palestinian staff asked us to talk to the troops at the road-blocks. As expatriates maybe we could influence them. The students feared their identity cards would be confiscated. A group of our students also wanted to return to their homes in Bethlehem. I walked up to one jeep where a green beret N.C.O. was giving a student a hard time. I watched the process in the semi-darkness. I talked to the soldiers explaining everybody was tired and wanted to go home. The student recognized my voice. "See Brother Patrick, what they do to us." They had him against the jeep looking at his books page by page with a torch. I thought there was another student there and put my arm around him saying to the soldiers that he could go. I suddenly realized the young man had a heavy weapon in his hand. I couldn't help but laugh. Later I undertook to walk a larger group of students home. The Bir Zeit people also got through the other side of the University.

There is a famous tree on the property of the University. In the first courtyard near the set of doors opening onto the main corridor is a short almost, ugly tree. It's known as the Senate Tree. Here on its small trunk are pinned all the Senate announcements calling for meetings, stoppages etc. One of the Sisters composed the following to the Christmas Carol tune "O Tannenbaum."

"O Senate Tree, O Senate Tree Announcing no more cla-asses,
You make your plans in secrecy and still remain a mystery.
O Senate Tree, O Senate Tree
Another lo-o-ng year pa-asses."

IX / DEMONSTRATIONS

Stress can be alleviated by a good sense of humour. Our party songs occasionally took the form of ditties to Christmas tunes. This was no disrespect to the sacredness of the season, but they did illustrate the reality of the human situation around us.

To the tune of "O little town of Bethlehem" sung with such peace and grace:

"O little town of Bethlehem,
How still we see thee lie
Until the flag of Palestine
Is hoisted to the sky..."

And then followed with vigour and urgency to the sound of Jingle Bells:

"Then: Soldiers come, students run,
Stones and tear gas fly.
Bethlehem University gates are
closed again.
Never reason why-y."
"While we wait, negotiate
Hoping all the while,
Weary days will have an end
With classes back in style."

The above doggerel was very close to the truth. Demonstrations were unexpected in the sense that the Senate kept them a secret. They did not want the military nor the administration to know. We knew that there would be disturbances around certain dates, particularly Balfour Day at the end of October or the beginning of November though the precise time and day were uncertain.

Classes then, would begin at 8:00 o'clock in the morning. You could often sense a certain unease by nine o'clock. If students thought a demonstration was imminent many would stay outside the property so as not to get caught inside.

It was the nine o'clock class which would present difficulties. One felt as though the students were on the starting blocks tensed up for a hundred meters sprint. In fact this was precisely what would happen. A member of the Student Senate would appear in a kiffiyeh and the Palestinian flag would be hoisted. This was like the starter's gun. The classes emptied with hundreds of students rushing for the gates, which by then were closed by the Student Senate. This was the only exit available for most students. Large numbers of staff would manage to get out via a passage at the back of the buildings near the hotel management department. Some students would desperately attempt climbing the walls near the School for the blind which adjoined our property. Most students were in fact caught between their obligations to attend class and their wish to be away from what followed. There were a number who wanted to stay, feeling they should show solidarity with the very small number who actually threw stones. Now during the Intifada, it is only a few young men between the ages of fourteen and twenty, who confront the soldiers. So with the demonstrations, I doubt if there were more than fifty young men and several women.

The beginning of a demonstration was always attended by the fear of the unexpected and a sense of hysteria. Young freshmen students were frightened and fearful wondering what was going to happen next. Groups of girls, often from the camps and sometimes wearing kiffiyehs to disguise themselves, ran around the campus placing buckets of water in strategic places. Piles of stones would appear, as if from nowhere. The administration always tried to have the stone walls well cemented down. Near the Brothers' house, girls were hurriedly pulling down one of our garden walls. There was no point in trying to stop them. The frantic intensity of the whole operation belied reasoning or argument. It was as if a volcano, long dormant, erupted and the administration and staff could only stand by and admit control was lost and events would take their course.

· My first experience of one of these political manifestations left me drained and exhausted by six o'clock in the evening. The adrenalin runs at a high rate, there is always the possibility that a serious tragedy could take place. There was the chance of personal injury and the fear that the soldiers would find some reason for entering the property. Some students would tell me they willingly stayed, they found it exciting. Others were resigned, and with a patient oriental frame of mind would wait until all was over. The organizers, members of the Senate and the political parties, were often students from the camps. I do really think, especially those from the camps, that they wanted to expose the student body, many of whom came from quite prosperous middle class families, to exactly what they, as refugees, experienced at the hand of the military occupation. Also those involved with the stone-throwing needed some security or cover at the end of the day. When finally the administration had negotiated with the Military Governor or his officers that the students could go home, those responsible for the disturbance could mingle with the hundreds that left the University.

There seemed, therefore, to be a pattern of events which accompanied these happenings. The Palestinian flag was highly illegal and therefore a challenge to the occupying force. Brother Joe, one of the earlier Vice- Chancellors at the beginning of the University's days did not understand or expect these demonstrations. Apparently a flag was placed on the bell-tower of the main building. He received a sharp telephone call from the Military Governor, who evidently could see it from his headquarters. "Get it down!" That was easier said than done. The individual that placed the flag had the ability of a mountain climber or steeple jack. With experience and hindsight all roof tops are sealed off with steel doors which, are permanently locked. Nevertheless, during the last series of demonstrations in October 1987, many students utilized the vast multi-purpose building which was still in the process of construction. The light doors were smashed by the students and a huge Palestinian flag placed on the roof. The red, green, white and black colours could be seen from Tantur and Mount Elias and with binoculars from Jerusalem. So the lines:

"Until the flag of Palestine is
hoisted to the sky"

had a certain significance to us. And it was during this initial phase of the day that I would go over to the Brothers' house, which was now located on the University property, to draw all the curtains, lock doors and windows. We, as a community, made the decision either to stay inside the house out of sight, or to be with the body of students on the campus as a presence. Most of us would stay with the large number of students who would eventually be crammed into the science building. Once the troops had arrived, this was probably the only place where tear gas had not penetrated.

"Round two" in the proceedings often began with a lull, once the earlier activity was completed. I recall on one occasion the troops did not turn up for over an hour. It seemed rather like the "phoney war" atmosphere experienced in England in 1940. On other occasions the troops arrived in force very quickly.

Generally the stone-throwing was more a symbolic gesture of defiance rather than a lethal weapon against the soldiers. The administration, had I believe, under the instructions of the Military Governor erected high railings on top of the already high walls, so it made it difficult for stone-throwers to be effective. Nevertheless the bangs that were associated with the tear gas firing would commence. The canisters would arch their way into the grounds. Screams and shouts would accompany the stampede for cover and safety away from the appalling gases. Canisters would fall near doorways, and the gases would float down corridors. Occasionally some canisters actually went into buildings. Those students actively engaged in the confrontation would try to put the canisters, before they exploded, into buckets of water. Others, who had gloves on, threw them back at the troops. I saw one young man, he would have won "the throw the cricket ball" competition at an English garden party, pick up a canister and launch it skywards in a parabola almost certainly sending it into the group of soldiers down Frères street. At the end of the day he proudly showed me his hand. The heat of the canister had made his hand one huge blister.

Tear gas can be very effective. On one occasion we counted five different types of canister. Some of them had round inflated rubber fixtures which made them bounce. Certainly the gases became more harmful as new types were used. During the last demonstration a large number of students were overcome by gas and were having quite serious breathing difficulties. Those students near the gas would often collapse. There would be dramatic rescue teams manhandling the unconscious or choking individual to the nursing school in the science block. I sometimes think that in their excitement more harm was done to the casualty in transit than by the gas. It was not uncommon to see heads hitting the ground. In one instance four frenzied men rushed one male student across the gardens, blind to the fact that there were small sturdy trees. The unfortunate individual, his legs held wide open by the two leading men rushed headlong into the trunk of the tree hitting him amidships. His rescuers, each holding a leg either side the tree suddenly drew up to a halt, their faces registering a momentary flash of incomprehension.

Our present Vice-Chancellor stays above ground. Key members of the administration use offices in the basement of the main building to keep in touch with the military. Serious injuries, hospital cases often require ambulances to enter the property through the army roadblocks. Difficult negotiations ensue, particularly as the students realize they will be immediately arrested. Brother Anton de Roeper, however, walks around the campus. Quite literally tear gas containers whiz pass his head and explode. You see him appear through a cloud of gases, stoically enduring fumes. Perhaps it is his English stiff upper lip or the fact that he comes from an army family. His father, I believe, was a colonel and one of his brothers fought in Korea was awarded the Military Cross. Once I pleaded "Anton, you look awful" his face was red and his eyes inflamed. "Yes," he said "it hurts, but I'm not complaining." Incidentally he sometimes mentions, not without a little historical pride, that his forebears were responsible for burning the British fleet in the Medway estuary near Chatham.

Just one last thing about the gases, which have attracted the attention of the medical world during the present Intifada, is the simple and surprising method of partially assuaging their discomforts: onions. A sliced onion held closely to the nose works wonders. Naturally large supplies of onions appear on campus and I spend much of my time cutting up small portions, as I wander round talking to the students. As the day draws on, the gases drift around the grounds. You cannot see the gases which are now invisible. I have encountered the gas sometimes days later caught in a sheltered area and permeating the fabrics for a longer periods of time.

Tragedy is always close at hand in these disturbances. Often the demonstration will end without serious injuries. Two years ago, a particularly severe colonel in charge of the military announced he would "have order in his land." He intended to enter the compound and arrest a third of the students. I happened to be in the main science lecture hall, where several hundred students were present. The Senate President stood on the demonstration dais and announced that the religious Brothers and Sisters would stand between the students and the soldiers. I don't actually recall making any promises to this effect but my arms were held high in the air by relieved students. Such are one's moments of fame! In fact it was all some-what frightening. Troops with guns, both male and female, used ladders to climb the walls, they carried large truncheons, and the situation looked grim. Fortunately, unknown to me at the time, the administration was making desperate communications with the Commander-in-Chief of the West Bank near Ramallah to prevent what could have been a blood bath, from occurring. Good sense on the part of the Israeli Commander won the day. It was not always easy for the University administration to negotiate with the Israeli occupying authorities. There seemed to be three different military officials for the Bethlehem area, one dealing with civil affairs, another with the purely military concerns and a third with security. During the disturbances at the University one, two or all three were involved and they did not always agree, or at least so it seemed.

For the students from the camps the disturbances were quite normal affairs. Stone throwing was so frequent at Deiheisha that fences thirty feet high were erected along the perimeter of the camp adjoining the Hebron Road. One individual jokingly called it the tennis net. To me it was just another symbol of treating the people like caged animals, and not human beings. At the end of one confrontation with the soldiers, it must have reached 5:30 p.m. in the evening, one of the students put his arm around my shoulders. He was a very likeable rogue, highly intelligent, who did a minimum amount of work academically because, as he said to me, "I have many commitments." He must have seen my weariness and glazed stare at the mess all around.

"Well Brother Patrick, we won, we beat them this time!"

The troops had withdrawn and the tired, hungry students were just about to walk through the gates. He was quick to see my hesitation in agreeing with him. After all, the result of the afternoon's chaos was at least a week's closure, numerous arrests with students missing their classes and returning later expecting special treatment. With that mischievous twinkle in his eye but on a serious note he said.

"Really, if you lived where I lived, if you saw your land taken from you, wouldn't you do the same?

It was hard to answer "no" to that question.

Inevitably tragedy did occur during one of these protests. Isac Abu Srur was shot in the head on October 28th 1987. The demonstration appeared to follow its usual sequence of events. What we did not realize at the time was the severity of the encounter with the soldiers in and around the multi-purpose building at the back of the property. This structure is a veritable fortress over looking Children's Street. Its flat roofs rise story after story. Its architecture is a bewildering series of levels and stairways with an indoor gymnasium and open-air amphitheatre. The protesting students gathered mainly in this area so the main building blocked a view of what was going on. From what I heard and a little of what I saw, not only was a large flag hoisted above the building but also several smaller flags on poles. The newspaper reporter for the Jerusalem Post, Joel Greenberg, said the students built road blocks, burnt logs and tar-filled barrels and taunted the troops. Certainly after the clash I saw the road covered in debris. What is not clear to me is why Isac should have been shot through the head. Apparently an officer had instructed a marksman with a 0.22 inch sniper rifle to fire at Isac. Shortly before Rodayna al Ayasseh, a woman student, was shot in her hip and several students were seriously overcome by tear gas. What I do know is that Isac was carried in through the door near the chapel. The blood spurting from his head, leaving a trail down the corridor. Frantic efforts were made in the nurses' area to revive him. Those present told me his heart stopped for twenty minutes. I believe he was virtually dead before he left by ambulance. Meanwhile a column of Border Police had run along the campus wall. There was a thunderous bang as a lobbed concussion grenade went off and further shots cracked into the air. I was standing in the main corridor when twenty to thirty students came from the multipurpose area enraged by what had happened. They entered classrooms ripping legs off chairs and smashing the notice boards. This happened in an intense exchange some time between midday and two o'clock. Isac was taken under arrest to the neurological department of the Hadassah Hospital, Ein Kerem.

I recall a sullen silence pervading the campus later in the afternoon and then a group of students stood in a circle joining hands, and singing filled the air softly at first and later with greater intensity.

So it was that Isac Abu Srur who sat at the back of my Shakespeare classes last semester struggling to learn some of the lines

"O speak again, bright angel for thou art..."

And learning such lines as:

"My bounty is as boundless as the sea.
My love as deep; the more I give to thee,
the more I have, for both are infinite."

This was the Isac I had picnicked with at Solomon's Pool and chatted to under the trees with his friends in the University gardens.

He died. He was twenty-one and would have graduated at the end of the academic year.

Under the desert night sky a small column of jeeps and a truck carried his body at 1:00 a.m. to its grave. Only his father and his mother and three other men of the family attended. They buried him, clawing at the stony ground with their bare hands while the area was cordoned by troops, near the monastery of St. Theodosius at a place called Obedih. The local bedouin took pride in caring for the shallow grave.

One month later, the Intifada began.

X / THE VOLCANO ERUPTS

W.B. Yeats, genius and prophet, ends his "Second Coming" with:

"And what rough beast, its hour come round at last,
Slouches towards Bethlehem to be born?"

Perhaps the explosion that took place in early December 1987, spreading from Gaza and into the West Bank, even reaching Bethlehem, was not "Surely some revelation is at hand" in the sense that W.B. Yeats intended. Yet it was, nevertheless a result from his description that

"Things fall apart; the centre cannot hold.
Mere anarchy is loosed upon the world."

Hindsight has a tendency to make us all wise men and women. Looking back, yes, I did detect a worsening of peoples' attitudes on the West Bank. Students at the beginning of the Autumn Semester 1987 were often uncharacteristically sullen. Maybe I was beginning to see more, understand just a little bit further, than before, how they felt. Then there was the hang-glider affair. This did bring some sense that the Israeli army was not as invincible as it appeared. The incident in Gaza early in December, where four local people were killed in a car accident at the Jabalya intersection five kitometres from Gaza city, probably more than anything ignited the uprising. Whether the Israelis had murdered the four Palestinians or not is still debated by some. What to me, was important, was the combustible situation David Grosman in his beautifully written book "The Yellow Wind" concedes, talking about the Israeli policies in Gaza and on the West Bank

"The history of the world proves that the situation we preserve here cannot last for long. And if it lasts, it will exact a deadly price."

Nevertheless the uprising was not expected at the time. The situation, to use the volcanic simile, was in some way like the people living in Martinique around Mount Pelee. The population of the city of Saint Pierre knew about the previous eruptions of the volcano and to some extent the volatile nature of the region.

In 1902 the explosion occurred, the cloud of incandescent ash wiping out the entire town of 30,000 persons within a few seconds. In the smouldering arena of Gaza and the West Bank and for that matter, the whole of the Middle East, the unpredictability of events is a key characteristic.

Our thoughts in Bethlehem University were overwhelmingly concerned with the closure resulting from the demonstration on October the 28th, that led to Isac Abu Srur's death. The next day we were expecting some decision from the military governor. One of the University staff telephoned to say he had heard on the Israeli military radio that Bethlehem University was to be closed for three months. In a land where rumour is rife, we waited in disbelief. Then we were quite stunned when military order 854 arrived. In a small brown envelope on rather poor paper was the note in Hebrew quoting the military order and closing us arbitrarily for three months. This devastating communication came at the end of October. During the next four weeks of November we were all shaken, trying to adjust our lives and also hoping that eventually through negotiation we may be able to reopen the University in mid-December. In the past, various punishments handed out by the occupying military government had been reduced. This is one of the one thousand two hundred military laws that have changed vast areas of life, in Gaza and on the West Bank.

My thoughts were also influenced by the reflections and fact finding of people like the Israeli researcher, Meron Benvenisti. Back in May 1987 I listened to his address at the Tantur Institute on the reality of the situation as he saw it and from the first hand information gathered by his West Bank Data Base Project. At the time, the world press spread rumours of international conferences. He argued, convincingly for me, that these were all a "game of procedure." That on "matters of substance, there is nothing to be discussed." "On the ground," he said, "Nothing will change." He said the struggle was for survival, and each side did not recognize the enemy. Everything was in absolutes. He did see the conflict as internally generated and continuing as intercommunal strife, a type of "twilight war," not the externally generated conflict of the past. He was correct in his analysis that "Intercommunal Strife" would continue with "trees, houses, stones" in the foreseeable future. What he did not predict was an uprising so intense and widespread.

Another factor, of a more personal nature, distracted me during the month of December. At 2:00 o'clock in the morning on 14th December, Bethlehem time, my sister Bridget telephoned to say my mother had died. By the 18th December I was flying home. We buried her on 22nd December, next to my father in the church yard of Saint Birinus in Dorchester-on Thames. In the Mass and funeral liturgy the opening singing was from "Once in Royal David's City." It seemed appropriate three days before Christmas to sing this Christmas carol.

For the family the passing of my mother, though a sad loss, was, if faith is "that with which we grasp the unseen, the uncertain," a celebration. Obviously, too, the carol related to where I was serving. But more importantly words conveyed to me the idea of motherhood and family.

"Mary was that Mother mild
Jesus Christ her little child."

When now I ride or walk over the bridge, which spans the narrow river Thames into Dorchester and I see the outline of Saint Birinus Church through the trees and the river below, I say the words of the poet:

"Sweet Thame, run softly while I sing my song."

I did not return to Bethlehem until the second week of January partly because flights were heavily booked, but also because there was family business to settle. On the telephone to Bethlehem I was told that Christmas was a depressing time. Obviously, the Midnight Mass celebrated by the Apostolic Delegate at the University could not be held. The entry of the Latin Patriarch into Bethlehem and the accompanying rejoicing and procession did not take place though Midnight Mass was said. The Times of London reported this. I was also informed over the telephone that the area experienced torrential rain. Apparently, three inches fell in the twenty-four hours before Christmas. The rainfall for 1987 totalled 37 inches for the Bethlehem area. London, if my memory serves me correctly, on average, receives 24 inches annually. Yes, 1987 was going to be a year to remember!

I arrived back to experience the joy of the Christian Palestinians, not just the Latin Christian Palestinians, in the appointment of Father Michel Sabbah, as the first native Palestinian Latin Patriarch. I was present at the procession to the Holy Sepulchre and his historical entry into Bethlehem. Later he had dinner with us in our house. He was, after all, and had been for several years, a close friend and President of Bethlehem University. We delighted in his intelligent, unobtrusive and friendly approach. His appointment gave heart to the Palestinians at a crucial time.

It was during this period that the uprising began to take on the form of a cohesive movement. It had started in a spontaneous way and in some measure remained so. And yet in January 1988 it began to show signs, at least to me who had just arrived back, of clever organization and a direct challenge to the military authority.

In January I wrote the following: "The familiar thumping beat of the rotor blades of a patrolling Israeli helicopter passes low over the roof tops of Bethlehem. The weather, promising in the morning, is now dull and wet. After a one day break the general strike on the West Bank resumes. The leaflets circulated by the National Palestinian Force call for a closure of all shops and stopping of public transport, and urge people to stay in their homes. The locals say there's been nothing like this since 1967. Apart from a few Arab vehicles splashing along Manger Street and Star Street everything is very quiet, grey and still.

The day before yesterday I saw at first hand the daily incidents in the shopping areas of Bethlehem. The shops are closed until the troops in jeeps with loud speakers order them to open. Talking to student friends in their shop, hastily opened after their parents telephoned to warn them the truck and crew with the welding equipment were coming their way, we saw the trucks with the oxyacetylene equipment. Shops not opened have the steel shutters and doors that cover the windows and entrances, sealed up. The shops are closed for 3 months and there is 6 months imprisonment for the owners if they attempt to open them. In some areas, shortly after the troops pass, groups of young Arabs smash the windows of shops that are open. Nearby we met a member of the University staff, a Palestinian, white with anger, harassed by constant threats and seething with indignation at the language used by the troops over their loud speakers.

"You Arab bastards, you'll lick the arse of the military governor" and so on. One shopkeeper, took us by the arm to show his shop sealed up, and close by, was a photographer's shop which was smashed up by the roving youths.

Earlier, James driving the Brothers' community mini-bus which has an Israeli number plate, was surrounded by youths who smashed the windscreen and started to block the road both in front and behind the vehicle with stones. This continued until adults understanding James' heated Arabic and display of the University signs, prevented further damage.

Many parents say that they are losing control over their children. They are obviously worried, and try to prevent the boys from leaving home. With some Christian families there was hardly any celebration at Christmas. A wife of a doctor, friends of the Brothers, explained that the military governor's office telephoned, ordering her husband to report to the military the following day. She said she would not tell her husband until the following morning: tension and uncertainty prevail. Meanwhile we wait, hoping the University will open at the end of January, though we remain very realistic that, if things continue as they are, it would be most unwise to do so. Yet as one Palestinian said who arrived on the West Bank from Gaza, "You people are in heaven compared to the hell suffered by the population in Gaza."

And later, because the University was closed and we lived isolated within its walls: "Several of us, frustrated with the inactivity, and closed up in the house, went for an afternoon walk in Bethlehem. It proved to be rather eventful. The

Beit Sahour and the Shepherds' Fields just east of Bethlehem.
The desert hills are in the background.

(see page 1)

Young Palestinian women are given the opportunity to study at university.

(see page 2)

An intensive English class. First year young men from refugee camps and villages.

(see page 12)

The end of the autumn semester 1986. An English class at Bethlehem University.

(see pages 17–20)

The statue of the child Jesus on the university clock tower.
One of the highest locations in Bethlehem.

(see page 46)

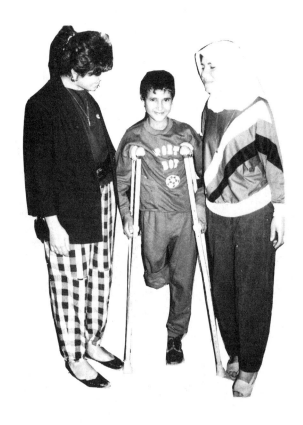

Suleiman, twelve years old, at the Rehabilitation Centre in Bethlehem.
He lost his right leg, the result of a dum dum bullet.

(see page 98)

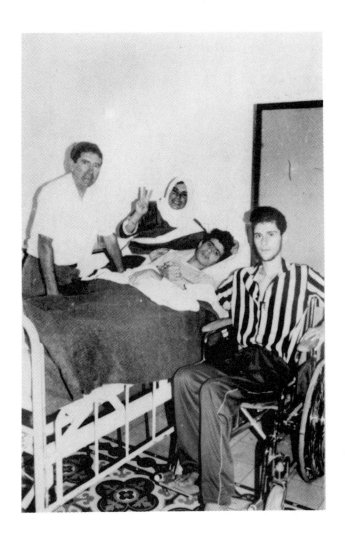

Brother James helps with basic physiotherapy.

(see page 98)

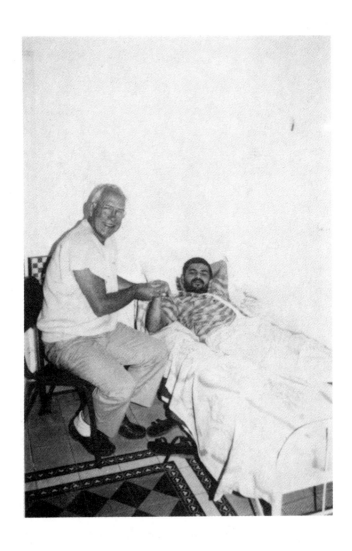

Brother Joe helps out at the Rehabilitation Centre.

(see page 98)

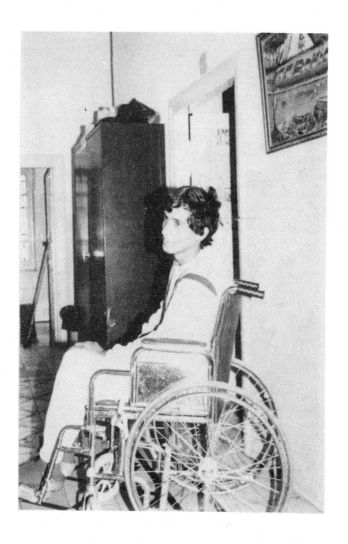

Jehad. Seriously wounded and in a wheelchair for the rest of his life.

(see page 98)

Nursing the young wounded Palestinians.
Yvette a married American Maryknoll volunteer.

When we were open. Christmas time 1986 in "The Harbour".
We had just put up the decorations.

A young Muslim woman student from a village on the
desert margin east of Bethlehem.

(see page 106)

entrance into Manger Square from Star Street was blocked by troops, who surrounded the Mosque, where apparently there was a demonstration. We went with an Arab newspaper reporter to the Square down a side alley. Dozens of police and soldiers had cleared the square. Tear gas, an all too familiar experience for us, hung in the air. Pilgrims, some Polish Catholics, were huddled against the walls of the Nativity church with an Israeli guide.

The Arabs in the Mosque were forced out: the women and then the men. Arrests were made. An ambulance took away an unconcious elderly man beaten on the head by troops or Shin Bet. We met one of the University staff who works in the computer room near to weeping. His brother and relatives were arrested. Apparently some Arabs had thrown stones. One of their relatives was shot twice in the neck and killed when he protested at the confiscation of his sheep. His house, apparently, was destroyed by the military according to the reporter. Edging our way around Manger Square, we met Mayor Freij's son, who invited us up to the Municipal offices. Br. Joe, as a former Vice-Chancellor, was well known, and we were invited to sit with the mayor. He was despondent and frustrated. He said the poor in Bethlehem were suffering hardships and, given another week or so, under these circumstances, there would be starving families. He asked Br. Joe if we could help. He had recently lunched with Mr. Mellor a few days previously and he was encouraged by his forthrightness. In particular while representing the British Government on his visit to Israel, Mr. Mellor confronted the Israeli military in Gaza with an incident of the beating and arresting of a young Arab. Earlier, from the Brothers' house and our bedroom windows we saw an Israeli bus stoned by youths. The bus was full of troops who swarmed up the slope from Manager Road to find the Palestinians. We saw patrols arrest young men below us."

It was later, after I arrived back that the phase of beatings by soldiers and security forces appeared on the TV screens of the world. I recall writing the following during the cold wet February.

"A cold wind and unpleasant driving rain added to the grey atmosphere of Manger Road. February often is a month to get through rather than savour. Closed shops, deserted streets, blustery low clouds and only the occasional traffic splashing and winding its way on the circuitous highway, made up the setting that day in Bethlehem. Little, featureless, vulnerable figures bent in the rain and scurrying about their business, or perhaps just seeking shelter, represented the sense of isolation and sadness of the moment. The English painter Lowry would have appreciated the scene. Strike days and curfews of the Intifada would have fired the satirical anger of his vision, if he had chanced to walk in Bethlehem.

Amongst the isolated, bent figures, were two Charles de Foucauld Sisters making their way home that afternoon. At one of the bends (there are many of them on Manger Road) down the entrance of a small alleyway they met a man beating a young Palestinian. The heavy set man doing the beating, was, they discovered almost immediately, a member of Shin Bet. The Shin Bet are plainclothes operatives of the Israeli secret police. The Italian Sister, Chiara, who hardly measures five feet high, is in her twenties, wearing her very simple grey blue dress and veil, challenged the man. "What are you doing? What has this man done?" This was the period during the Intifada when beatings with truncheons were a common and widespread reaction from the military authorities. The courage of the young Sister in making this demand was considerable. I know of several instances when the punishment was applied to the person making the intervention.

The Shin Bet reacted quickly and fiercely. He took the young man by the scruff of the neck and ordered the diminutive figure of the Italian and the other Sister to the Police Station. They were marched along Manger Road up the hill that leads to Manger Square and into the police station, which dominates one side of the area.

In the police station the man took the young Palestinian into another room leaving the Sisters stranded in front of, I imagine, somewhat puzzled policemen and soldiers. They held their ground and made their representations to the officials. Later the Shin Bet returned with his prisoner. He declared in front of the group and the Sisters that he had not beaten the man. The little Sister answered immediately. "You beat him!"

The secret policeman then turned to the young man. "Did I beat you?" The Palestinian said he was not beaten or harmed. Then the Italian, more determined than ever said, "You beat him and you know that you beat him!"

Later that afternoon, three figures left the Police station in Manger Square. The two Sisters walked out into the early evening to return to their small simple dwelling and their work amongst the poor Moslem Arabs of Bethlehem. The third figure was the young Palestinian man who walked home free, without further bodily harm.

I would like to think that day in Bethlehem there was a certain beauty, which I think Lowry saw also in his vision, of those three figures as they departed on their way. And what about the human beings in the police station? Maybe, they dismissed the whole affair as something quite trivial, a day-to-day experience, a nuisance, a further complication in the whole nasty business of policing the uprising. There are, after all, innumerable ways of looking at the same events and dramas of life. Lowry saw the industrial sprawl around Manchester and the people in it. He said somewhere "I see what's going on in the world, and I don't think much of it, really."

What I had seen when I was in London on the British TV and, in Bethlehem, I now witnessed first hand. I was amazed by the coverage of the situation in the press and TV and I saw Mr. Mellor's now famous or infamous confrontation, according to your point of view, with the Israeli soldier. I do not recall the name "Intifada" been given to the uprising at the time. It may well have had the name by then, but it did not come to my attention as far as I remember. As events unveiled themselves in the day-to-day chaos and uncertainty, I became aware of what the Intifada began to mean, not just to the minority of the population, but to what I think became a national movement.

XI / THE MOVEMENT IS RECOGNISED: "THE INTIFADA"

As the events of the weeks accumulated the long-term seriousness of the situation became apparent. This, however, did not prevent, in February 1988, the whole faculty from being assembled and the Vice-Chancellor wanting to know whether they could advise him on the reopening of classes in the University. I remember various opinions were expressed. We tried to open a few days later. It was obvious to me that the classes between 9:00 a.m. and 11:00 a.m. were held in an unreal atmosphere. It was extraordinary that the campus was so quiet and peaceful, whereas in many parts of Bethlehem demonstrations were taking place from as early as 7:00 a.m. in the morning, well before the students arrived. Whatever element of the Intifada flourished on the campuses of the Universities over the years, it had now clearly fled and taken to the streets. That evening Brother Anton de Roeper, the Vice-Chancellor, was summoned to the military headquarters at about 8:00 o'clock; we were both watching television. He returned later to say we were closed indefinitely. In our hearts, though we did not say it openly, we realized we would not be able to operate for a long time to come. It was at this time that I first heard the term, Intifada.

What does Intifada mean? Apparently the word stems from the Arabic root "nafada." Words have different meanings. "Nafada" can mean to shudder, shiver, tremble. It can also describe, to shake off, shake out, dust off, and further meanings include "to recover, to recuperate to jump to one's feet." I am told, and later gradually became aware of, the significance of the meaning of the word. The first two meanings were evident describing the shudder or explosion needed to shake off the twenty-one years of military occupation. Not so obvious was the third process involving a reawakening, a cleansing and an inward attempt by the Palestinians to reformulate their identity, to start building structures, to recover to virtually be self-sufficient.

It is not my intention to say any more about the theoretical and political complexities of the uprising, but to illustrate the main events of the Intifada through the people and the events of their lives. Nevertheless from the events I describe the various elements of the Intifada can be identified.

Roughly about the time of Latin Easter, around early April, I wrote the following: "Almost imperceptibly the spring heat is here after the prolonged winter rains. The desert is still green, the slopes tall with grass in places and coloured by masses of spring flowers. Israeli spring time sees us rise an hour earlier. News of the Grand National and of Liverpool versus Nottingham Forest in the semi-finals of the FA Cup now comes to us over the BBC World Service, three hours behind. Shultz has completed his second shuttle. Nothing changes on the ground.

One of the graffiti in Arabic still disfiguring the new limestone walls of our multi-purpose building reads, in large red letters: "Sorry, Jesus, we can't celebrate your feast this Christmas." Well, that's some time ago-now. Bethlehem University is well into its sixth month of closure and has just received a further military order that it must stay closed until 8 May.

The uprising, spontaneous and widespread, battles on. As tension and frustration increase, the Israeli responses get tougher. Most of the brothers in the community listened to the Exsultet sung in St. Ann's church in the Old City at the Easter Vigil. "Let this place resound with joy, echoing the song of all God's people!"

We returned from St. Ann's to cross back into the West Bank and found ourselves virtually cut off for three days. In the dark near Tantur the road-blocks remained and passports were necessary, shown to shadowy figures silhouetted against the oil-burning flares. Bethlehem was a ghost town. Turning our mini-bus into Children's Street at midnight we must have alarmed a helmeted heavily-armed patrol of six. Israeli number-plates are a blessing in such circumstances. "This is our passover feast, this is our passover feast!" How difficult to analyse one's thoughts and emotions in this land of contradictions.

Events in Bethlehem over the past months of March and April reflect the deepening crisis. This tourist town, almost a satellite of thriving Jerusalem, has changed. We are beginning to see something of what Nablus, Ramallah, Hebron, Gaza and scores of isolated villages have suffered. Four of us had just returned from Amman on a Sunday morning. From our house we could see and hear below us rapid shooting and extensive military activity on Manger Road. The fast travelling rumour was later confirmed. A soldier was shot dead outside the administrative building and scores of troops moved into the area. Columns of Palestinians were arrested, escorted and put against the wall for detention and interrogation. All the shops on both sides of the road were sealed up, and the road barred by barbed wire and fencing for several weeks.

The spontaneity and suddenness of the clashes on the West Bank and Gaza Strip are well illustrated by a recent confrontation in Bethlehem. As part of the battle of wills in their attempt to crush the uprising, the troops were forcing the shopkeepers in the market to close. In protest young men threw stones. On the steps outside the Syrian Orthodox church, Saleem Shaer was shot dead. Central Bethlehem became a battlefield and fury spread through the streets, including Manger Square. Continuous gunfire and tear gas sent shoppers scurrying back into their homes.

Spontaneous too was the funeral. By noon the family had recovered the body of Saleem and in a rush of emotion and energy hundreds of men, women and children, some say over a thousand, joined the surging mass of people. The young man's mother soaked her white headscarf in her son's blood and the blood-stained body was carried high on a stretcher through the streets of Bethlehem. The procession went past the cinema, down Children's Street near the University towards the mosque at Azza Camp, and then across the Hebron main road to the cemetery adjoining Aida Camp. Helicopters repeatedly thundered over the house, and the funeral was bombed with tear gas and stones from the air.

Virtually all the shops are closed all day every day in Bethlehem now. Seeking a haircut, Tom managed to slip in behind the closed steel doors of Karim's shop. He almost suffered the loss of an ear when soldiers hammered on the doors just as the barber accomplished the final flourishes with his cut-throat razor. Cyril also had a similar experience when the barber switched the lights off as soldiers stopped outside and later in the proceedings retreated upstairs to a bedroom when the patrol returned. Patrick landed up in someone's kitchen surrounded by cross-legged children looking up with moon-like eyes as their father, who insisted that he knew how to cut hair, completed an excellent job for five shekels.

People now buy and sell in their homes. Cars and vans suddenly draw up and set up shop. In Beit Sahour the inhabitants are using their plots of land to plant vegetables. Money is restricted across the Jordan and the University staff have not received their salaries this month. All international telephone lines are cut and so too are many of the local lines. Journalists seeking to collect news are not allowed access, censorship is much tighter. Harassment and brutality continue unabated. Soldiers at New Gate in Jerusalem interrogate any Arab youths and are seen taking them off for a beating.

The Palestinians, stunned, spend the day listening to news on the radio and television. Children remain at home for there is no school. On visiting a family in Beit Sahour which had demonstrations every day, the wife was asked where her husband and son were. Humorously, but with some truth, came the reply. "They are out at the front!" The mind, traumatised, slows down. Something that would usually take thirty minutes to complete now takes an hour.

Joe and Patrick visited the village of Beit Ummar and Deiheisha Camp a few weeks ago. Both places have many students from the University. Beit Ummar, a rural village of remarkable beauty, lies north of Hebron and is surrounded by Israeli settlements. It had just been savaged by Israeli settlers as well as the army. We were guests of one of our students, in his fourth year in the English department. It was a harrowing experience visiting the three families whose sons had been shot dead, and another where, miraculously, a young man survived, though with a bullet lodged in his head which could not be operated on. Hiding in the houses were up to 30 people with smashed limbs. A young eight year old boy proudly showed where a bullet had gone through his arm—fortunately, it was a clean wound. Bulldozers had charged through the village clearing debris and barriers, but also smashing walls and gateways and damaging buildings.

In Deiheisha one of our students took us round as we visited students' homes. Not surprisingly, there were few young men around. Hundreds were in prison. Unofficially some estimate the number in prison in the occupied territories at 15,000. Others were in hiding or in hospital. Parents said their ten year old sons were "like time-bombs." If they were out in the alleys they would clash with troops. If they came home, troops arrived and beatings followed. In the camp near the University an eight year-old boy had his arms broken in front of his mother, to teach him in advance not to throw stones. Families in the centre of Deiheisha complained that they could get little sleep, for troops remained on their roofs during the night.

Maybe I should take another look at the fresh edition of graffiti on the walls of Bethlehem. Would we could see "Christ, our Morning Star which never sets, came back from the dead to shed his peaceful light on all mankind." Faith is that confident assurance concerning what we hope for, and conviction about things we do not see. So let's cry "Exsultemus"—"let us rejoice." The stars look so beautiful in the clear desert sky these days.

XII / A REAWAKENING AND SELF HELP

DOCTOR JAD

Before I left for the United States I became aware of the third element in the Intifada. This was the process of reawakening, cleansing and an inward attempt on the part of the Palestinians to reformulate their identity, to start building new structures, to recover, to virtually be self sufficient. During the months of April and May I saw for myself examples of the formation of committees which would attempt to organise this process. The story of Doctor Jad and his "Shed" in Beit Sahour is just one example. The vigour with which the Israeli authorities eventually crushed his efforts demonstrates their fear that the Palestinians were in fact attaining a measure of independence and autonomy the military occupation had always denied them.

I think I really started to get to know Doctor Jad on the University tennis courts. Those were good days when after classes we would play doubles in the sunny, spring evenings. One of his younger children used to come along kitted-out in the national English football team colours. Apparently both father and son were keen soccer supporters and because of their long stays in England—Jad completed his doctorate in Biology at the University of East Anglia—they had almost a vested interest in the 1st Division and the national team. I could understand their enthusiasm for Norwich City—the "Canaries"—but was puzzled by the interest in the inconsistencies of the England team. Anyway, Jad's son was very keen, even to the extent of attempting to convert the sacredness of the tennis courts into a football pitch.

Doctor Jad was a man of positive enthusiasms. He had quite a dynamic character and quite strong opinions which he would quite readily express. Up until 1986 he was Dean of Sciences at Bethlehem University. The Deans rotate so that after 1986 he became a member of the science teaching faculty. His energy was involved, for sometime, in editing the Bethlehem University Journal and in initiating the first Palestinian Ecology Conference at the University. Though he liked academic work, he felt that the University tended to be an ivory tower, isolated from the surrounding community and not really meeting some of the more urgent needs. His enthusiasms included a strong interest in community out- reach. He was largely responsible for animating the community service programme and for preaching self- reliance schemes to the students. He gave talks in the Harbour and elsewhere on these topics. For a long time he was involved with a number of organizations that encouraged self-help. Various schemes for growing crops, particular types of plants, trees and rearing of livestock, poultry, rabbits etc, were of particular interest to him. He became increasingly concerned about setting graduates up in business and would, through a number of agencies, finance these. I believe I remember him encouraging graduate students to set up a bakery in Beit Sahour.

Apart from his enthusiasms for encouraging, particularly young Palestinians to become self-reliant economically, Jad's infectious energy showed itself in his approachability and friendliness. He was, I think, an anglophile, which of course meant there were few barriers for me to negotiate. I worked with him in my campus concerns area regularly. We organized a very successful University staff, students and family outing and had others planned. He was also full of ideas for creating community on campus. He was willing to give of his time. On several occasions I visited his house in Beit Sahour where we met his wife and children and his extended family. So Doctor Jad was a vocal man of action. When the Intifada developed he saw many opportunities to carry out his ideas of community self- help.

The town of Beit Sahour in which he was born, bred and now lives, is located on the site of the Biblical Shepherd's Field. From Bethlehem, this once village, and now town, spreads itself out from the lower slopes of the hills which constitute the ground on which Bethlehem developed. Beit Sahour's 9000 population have built their houses almost to the fringe of the desert. Most of the population are Christians. Unlike other Christian communities in the Occupied Territories, from which large numbers of residents have emigrated—Ramallians to California and Bethlehemites to Latin America, for example, Beit Sahour has no emigration problem. Here residents have remained. They are highly educated. The percentage of university graduates among them is the highest in the West Bank. Beit Sahour provides, therefore, the Bethlehem area as well as other parts of the Occupied Territories with teachers, university professors, doctors, engineers, and other professional and business people.

The residents of Beit Sahour have always been deeply involved in education, industry, and trading, while being less concerned with agriculture, despite possessing a considerable area of good, fertile land. Moreover, they were active in social and cultural matters even before 1967. They founded sports and cultural clubs, societies, and committees of women, youth, and workers. Their neighborhood patterns have naturally united them in cooperating to organize the social activity of Beit Sahour, for the residents live in neighbourhoods composed, usually, of close relatives. There are as many as 30-40 neighbourhoods of family members in the town.

Doctor Jad was long accustomed to growing up in an environment where widespread and effective social and cultural activities, strong family ties and united neighbourhoods form a proud loyalty to the town of Beit Sahour. This environment was also associated with a strong political consciousness. Many of the political leanings of the people of Beit Sahour followed the more extreme left views of the PLO. This strong sense of identity furthered the spirit of initiative which was so well expressed in Doctor Jad's energies.

1) Because of the resignation of Arab policemen, there is no official protection for persons or property.
2) Children have been denied their right to receive an education with the long closure and then the early reclosure of the schools.
3) The number of poor families is rising exponentially.
4) There has been collective punishment: economic pressures, check-points, road blocks, transportation limitations, and curfews.
5) Work, trade, and industry have been greatly disrupted and disordered.
6) A high number of residents have been arrested.
7) Violent clashes between youths and soldiers have led to the punishment, harrassment, and humiliation of innocent people.

Faced with these new realities, the residents of various neighborhoods in Beit Sahour took action that was not forbidden by any existing laws in the region. They provided the following responses to the situation:

1) Unarmed home guards protecting people and property,
2) Families planting their own backyard gardens with vegetables,
3) Lectures given to the community on First Aid,
4) Food, medicine, and First Aid equipement gathered and stored,
5) Poor families given assistance,
6) Open home schools educating the children,
7) Voluntary work teams trained to help in cleaning the streets of Beit Sahour.

At the same time, doctors of Beit Sahour started a low-cost medical treatment programme, merchants announced fixed and lowered prices for various goods, social societies and clubs raised funds to help needy families, and a group of professionals, including agricultural engineers, established an agricultural centre to provide the local community with seeds, seedlings, and agricultural equipment.

It was at the agricultural centre that Doctor Jad could help, lead and provide expertise. It seemed only natural, he would be involved in what was a perfectly legitimate activity. In fact, on a smaller scale he was already doing this. All the people in Beit Sahour were convinced that having suffered under the restrictions of the occupation authorities since early in the uprising, especially under harsh economic pressures, they came to realize the value of using their land to grow vegetables and other kinds of plants and saw the urgent need to cooperate in doing this work for the sake of their survival. There was an unanticipated enormous response to an agricultural centre set up in the community. The story of "The Shed" as it came to be called, is an example of one of Beit Sahour's responses to the situation.

Doctor Jad was one of five founders of the "Shed" which I visited one day in April 1988. Jad explained with his usual enthusiasm the early activities setting up "The Shed." The group of friends who established the centre had, for many years, shared a love of gardening. They decided to provide agriculture supplies and services to neighbours at reasonable prices.

The group first purchased some seeds and seedlings from a nursery in Jericho. Then they distributed these to their friends and relatives. When others heard about the availability of seeds and seedlings, they came to the group asking for such supplies. Since the demand continued to grow, the group next decided to operate a centre formally in order to provide these agricultural needs. A friend, in Beit Sahour, generously gave the use of a piece of land with a shed on it to the group, hence the name, "The Shed." Each member of the group then chipped in some money to raise the required capital to start operating. The demand grew still greater. People came to "The Shed" asking for pesticides, fertilizers, and irrigation equipment. The group then decided to enlarge their business.

Doctor Jad then drove us round Beit Sahour to see the scheme in action. We had already seen "The Shed" with its surrounding land stored with all the equipment for irrigation, fertilizers, seeds and tools. Each neighbourhood seemed to have its own cultivated area. According to Doctor Jad, since 13th March 1988, 200,000 seedling of tomato, eggplant, pepper, cauliflower and lettuce were sold at 1.8 shekels for 20 seedlings per packet. More than 150 kilograms of seeds of cucumber, summer squash. beans, raddishes etc, were sold. About 1000 fruit trees also were purchased and planted. I saw the fields, scientifically irrigated with drip equipment. More than 40,000 metres of black rubber tubing were sold. With all this the fields were fertilized and pesticides also carefully applied. Liquid compound fertilizers were introduced for the first time in this area.

Then having seen the fairly large fields—it reminded me of the medieval three field system with the involvement of a whole neighbourhood in sharing crops and land on one field—we visited the gardens and small holdings where we saw the families who had purchased some of the 2000 layer chickens, the 2000 fryer chickens and eight high quality Assaf lambs. Cages also had been supplied. With all this went the free advice of the experts that travelled around giving help.

It soon became clear that the work of this group fulfilled a vital and urgent need in Beit Sahour. The increasing demands by residents on "The Shed" could not be met by the volunteer work of the group members and their families and helpers alone. Consequently, one person was employed on the 23rd of March 1988, to assist in sales. Soon it was further realized that extension services were greatly needed by the community; an agricultural engineer was employed on the 1st of April to assist in its extension work. Later, when "The Shed" started offering its services to other areas, the group employed a third person to meet the growing demand on the centre.

The growth of the services of the centre continued. The group was working as a liaison between rabbit and pigeon breeders in the community and those who wanted to start such projects.

The demand seemed to be far greater than the supply, so the group was considering having its own rabbitry to provide good quality breeds to the community. The group also intended to launch a campaign to eradicate the olive fly which has seriously damaged this important crop, but this year olive trees seem to be doing exceptionally well and, thus, the campaign was postponed.

I had left for my work in the United States at the beginning of May. It was the last I saw of Doctor Jad. "The Shed" closed its doors on 5th of June 1988 by military order from the authorities. I only gathered later, when I returned in early September 1988, that dramatic events had taken place in Beit Sahour and that Doctor Jad was imprisoned for six months.

Before the arrest of Doctor Jad it became clear that the effects of these community efforts were amazing. They provided a practical model demonstrating that cooperative social work based on a home economy can provide self-protection through self-help for the people during unstable political situations. What was happening in Beit Sahour was a positive beginning in escaping from the circle of violence and in entering into an avenue of negotiation. The activities of Beit Sahour even encouraged other areas likewise to initiate non-violent activities rather than to continue violent street clashes. "Beit Sahour is an inspiring example to all of us Palestinians," said one man from the Ramallah area.

The Jerusalem Post described the resistance of Beit Sahour as "a quiet kind of uprising." And this is true, for even massive protests there could not be described as violent. They usually started as a peaceful demonstration in which women and old people as well as men, youth, and girls participated. The reason that some of those demonstrations resulted in violent confrontations between the youth and the army was the excessive force used by soldiers to disperse the demonstrators.

Hundreds of journalists were crowding the Occupied Territories during the spring, looking for fresh stories in the uprising. Many of them saw that the activities in Beit Sahour as well as in other areas added a new dimension to the struggle between the residents of the territories and the occupation authorities. Journalists began covering these activities, bringing them to world attention. The people of Beit Sahour helped them to show that Palestinians are committed to building and organizing their community life, not just to resisting the occupation violently. The activities of Beit Sahour residents indeed gave a model of peaceful resistance rather than one which would result in deepening the hostility between the two nations.

Doctor Jad was often involved in explaining the schemes to the visiting journalists. From what happened following this publicity was a clear indication that the military authorities were none too pleased. Two episodes followed which illustrated the occupying power's determination to crush any organized or cohesive activities by Palestinians however legal.

First was the episode of harassment that lead to the closure of the agricultural centre. On four separate occasions, Dr. Jad Isaac, three others involved with "The Shed" were summoned by Captain Yaron, the advisor on Arab Affairs at the Bethlehem Military Headquarters. They were individually questioned about their agricultural business in Beit Sahour. On each occasion they stated repeatedly that they were a close group of professionals who had two things in common: an old friendship and a love of gardening. Their decision to start an agricultural business in Beit Sahour stemmed from a simple desire to supply agricultural materials and provide agricultural services to the community. Two other shops in Bethlehem provided services similar to theirs; it was not something strange.

On the 17th of May 1988, the deputy military governor in Bethlehem, Major Mufeed Salah, together with Captain Yaron, accompanied by scores of soldiers, stormed the house of Jad Isaac at 4:30 pm, and arrested him in a theatrical manner that seemed designed to scare the members of his family, especially his children. He was kept in a cell until 12:30 after midnight without being questioned. He was then released and left to walk home.

On the 1st of June 1988, Jad Isaac and one of the other organizers were summoned to the military government headquarters at 8:00 a.m. They were seen first by Captain Yaron and later by Major Mufeed. They were accused of being members of a popular committee and told that their agricultural activities were "political" and dangerous, both to the people and to the security of the area. Both of them denied those allegations completely. They said they were law- abiding citizens who had no records whatsover with the authorities. They declared, further, that they understood that a popular committee is one which is elected or appointed by the people; they, on the other hand, had "appointed" themselves to run this enterprise. Major Mufeed, at a later time, threatened both with 24-hours military surveillance at their homes and anywhere they went.

Other threats included imprisonment and long-term detention. Major Mufeed insisted that the agricultural business must be stopped immediately; otherwise, harassment would continue. This ordeal concluded at 6:25 pm, of the same day.

The harassment grew. On that same day, the 1st of June, 1988, soldiers unexpectedly erected a checkpost right outside of Dr. Isaac's house. They deliberately made noisy U- turns on the one-way street with their military vehicles in the middle of the night. If this did not awaken the inhabitants of the house, strong flashlights beamed into the bedroom windows ensured that they did. Needless to say, the events of that day and the following ones were terrifying for the families and children. Further harassment was the disconnecting of the telephones. On the 5th of June 1988, Jad and two others were again summoned for 8:00 a.m.

They received the same treatment as previously, waiting until 4:30 pm. Before they were allowed to go home, a certain Captain Yuval came to the room where they had been kept with a few other people. He gave them a lecture on how to behave. The men, being law-abiding citizens who did not want any confrontation with the authorities and who wanted to alleviate the sufferings of their families, decided to listen to the advice of the mayors of Bethlehem and Beit Sahour, who had interceded on their behalf. They closed "The Shed" on the 5th of June, 1988.

On the 6th of June, 1988, at 8:30 a.m. the men appeared again at the military government headquarters where they stayed until 2:00 pm. At that time they were seen by the military governor and Captain Yaron. They were again warned not to be involved in political activities or in popular committees or to consult or to advise about gardening with anyone. They were threatened with vague consequences and with constant surveillance. They were told to sign a statement to that effect, which is what they did before they were given their ID cards back. Most ironically, Dr. Isaac was told to remove the symbol of a "front" organization from his house. This so-called symbol is the emblem of the Star of Bethlehem with a meteor, put on his house which is located in Shepherds' Field at the time of its construction in 1982!

The second episode in the spate of harassment against Beit- Sahour residents crested on Thursday, July 7th, 1988, a day of showdown and suffering.

Tax collectors and soldiers raided Beit Sahour at 4:30 a.m. They blocked off streets, detained owners of cars and other residents at the Beit Sahour Secondary School. They made a house-to-house search and broke into business premises. They confiscated Identity Cards.

In mid-morning the residents of Beit Sahour gathered inside and in front the Municipality Building to discuss the situation. In protest against the harsh tax raids, they agreed to return their Identity Cards to the military authorities though the Deputy Mayor. At about 11:00 am, the Deputy Mayor and the Military Governor were to have begun negotiations. The crowd was sent away and told to return at 4:00 pm, to hear the results.

The Deputy Mayor asked Dr. Jad Isaac, who had been at Bethlehem University and been unaware of the morning's events, and other residents known for their moderation to come to the Municipality Building in the early afternoon to discuss the situation. The people gathered again at 4:00 pm, more than two thousand of them. They were informed that the Deputy Mayor had had no negotiations with the authorities, that he had been cheated. Soldiers then ordered the people to disperse. The people, instead of dispersing as they had done earlier in the day, simply sat down on the street. They showed no violent reaction.

The soldiers dealt with this disobedience by arresting people and by suddenly opening fire with rubber bullets and tear-gas bombs directed into the crowd. The horrified and choking people ran away. Some of them, including Dr. Isaac, sought protection inside of the Municipality Building. Soldiers rushed after them into the building. One of the officers ordered Dr. Isaac to help disperse the people. He asked people to leave; some of them agreed to do so, and he and they walked out of the building. At that point Dr. Isaac was arrested. The authorities imposed a curfew on Beit Sahour.

In a legal affidavit, the Deputy Mayor, Khalil Khair, expressed deep dismay about Dr. Issac's cruel arrest. His moderate and balanced effort to quiet the situation made at the Deputy Mayor's request should have been rewarded by respect and gratitude, not by unjust arrest. At 3:00 a.m. Dr. Isaac was released after having been interrogated for an hour and a half. The next day, on Friday, July 8,1988, at 4:30 pm, he was arrested in his home. The family was later informed that he was being held in administrative detention for six months.

The authorities informed his lawyer, unofficially, about the charges that resulted in Dr. Isaac's arrest. First, they claimed that Dr. Isaac had threatened the mayor of Beit Sahour and told him to resign so that he himself could take his place. Second, they claimed that he is a member of a popular committee which is linked to an illegal organization. Third, they claimed that he was responsible for all of the acts of violence that occurred on Thursday afternoon. Lastly, they claimed that Dr. Isaac was the leader of the uprising in the Bethlehem area.

As for the first claim, the mayor of Beit Sahour is ready to write a declaration attesting that Dr. Isaac has never threatened him and that he is a good friend of his. As for the second claim, Dr. Isaac, was only involved in opening a private agricultural nursery which he had been forced to close by the authorities. As for the third claim, there had been no violence by the people of Beit Sahour on Thursday afternoon. The last claim is the most serious one. Everyone, including the authorities, knows that the leadership of the uprising is a coalition among organizations like Fateh, PFLP, DFLP, and so on. Speaking about Dr. Isaac as the leader of the uprising is ridiculous. Dr. Isaac has never been involved in politics and has never been linked with any illegal organization or action. He appears to have been the victim of propaganda that made some authorities angry with him and they decided to punish him. It is an arbitrary usage of administrative detention in the Occupied Territories.

So ended the venture with "The Shed." In addition to Doctor Jad's arrest six other prominent members of the Beit Sahour community were arrested. A ten day curfew was imposed in the town and at the end a young Palestinian was killed by a rock that fell from a roof where an army lookout was located. Huge demonstrations resulted and another seven days curfew was imposed.

During the total seventeen days of curfew, the crops in the fields were unattended and in the June heat most of them perished.

These are the facts as I gathered them from, what I believe to be, reliable sources. Doctor Jad is still in prison. His wife is not allowed to see him; only his lawyer. He will apparently be in prison out in the Negev for another two and a half months.

I am not sure whether the emblem of the Star of Bethlehem is still in place near the gables of Doctor Jad's house. For me the Star over Bethlehem signifies faith and hope for better things. Jad, in his enthusiasms, had faith and hope in his people and a confidence that they could do well together. Like those visiting astrologers to Bethlehem two thousand years ago, he observed the Star at it rising and rose, as it were, to its challenge.

XIII / BLIGHTED ANNIVERSARY

"Eight-Hundred and Seven Summit Avenue is where in Saint Paul, Minnesota, I stayed for a week. The Avenue runs east-west, parallel to Route I-94, and almost links the crests of the huge meander loops of the Mississippi as it cuts its way between the Twin Cities. Everything is a picture of order and peace. Well mown lawns slope down to the quiet sidewalks, a variety of trees in new green foliage proclaims the 'bounty overplus' of the Midwest spring. The mansions set back, grand and diverse in design, are a sign of the economic prosperity of the railway and lumber barons of a century ago. The wide pavements facilitate more joggers than pedestrians. Slim-line youths join middle and old age bones methodically thumping down on the paving slabs. And the cars glide through the avenue, small compacts and an increasing number of middle sized to larger vehicles—perhaps petrol is cheaper now—but anyway the American dream must go on. All is in order. All has its place. Even the driving is without frantic haste, and appears disciplined and courteous. For the European, the Midwest is a discovery. We know about the East and West coasts of the U.S. In our geography lessons we mapped out the dendritic patterns of the giant Mississippi and its tributaries. But ask us to locate or slot on the map the Gopher State of Minnesota and its neighbour Wisconsin, and we will have difficulty. Ask us to fill in the states of North and South Dakota or Iowa, we will hesitate vaguely, knowing they are not as far southwest as New Mexico, or Central West as Colorado. Somewhere in the middle, we would say, somewhere in the vast interior, somewhere west of the Great Lakes. Anyway, everything seems a far cry and distance from the less than orderly West Bank from which I have come."

I had arrived in the United States in mid-May. Nevertheless I continued to think back to the faces I left behind. I wrote, if I remember correctly, from a bay window that overlooked the Avenue, the following: "In my prayers these days, when the mind is at rest, the subconscious presents before my imagination faces, Palestinian faces. I cannot help remembering the words of a friend of mine, a Palestinian on the staff of Bethlehem, Moin Halloun, who in the midst of frustration and turmoil, said, "I love my students." We have missed teaching them for over seven months.

Yousef, a man in his thirties, fifteen years in prison, married now and his wife expecting her first baby. He is worried as to how he will feed and care for them, as the price of food rises and his wife stops working as a nurse at the Caritas Hospital. He only manages to earn a few shekels in the evenings at the Tantur Institute. He is in his third year at the University. And Jamal, bright, articulate, a senior in our science department, who, through fear and apprehension, sits on his bed fully clothed, dreading the arrival of troops bursting into the house as they systematically arrest young men in their homes in his area. Of Maysoun, a bright freshman from Bani Na'im, east of Hebron, struggling to recover from a gunshot wound in her thigh that exploded, breaking her femur and cutting the nerves. X-rays, so her doctor clinically describes, show the devastating effects of dum-dum bullets inside the human body. A face, too, I cannot mention her name, of one of our graduates—bright, attractive, personable, but unemployed and seemingly without hope—who, on having to report to the military, was instructed to meet with the Shin Bet in Jerusalem hotel. The Israeli man and woman offered her a job working for a Kuwait Business in West Germany. She speaks three languages, including German. In return, they wanted information about Kuwait. Three times she was ordered to various hotels, three times she refused the offers. As I sit here looking out into the Avenue, perhaps it is because of an association of ideas or circumstances that I hear the haunting voice of Meryl Streep in the film "Out of Africa" speak with controlled emotion but longing, looking back at her life. "I had a farm in Africa," she said.

Dare I recall, "I had taught Palestinians in Bethlehem?" Peres is in the U.S.A., and on TV last night he worried about the Silk Worm Missiles in Saudi Arabia, and with twisted logic and verbal gymnastics, justified the deportation of men from the village of Beita.

Just after the celebration of the fortieth anniversary of Israel we continued on what developed into an outreach to students, visiting camps and villages in April 1988.

"Nouh, our guide, protector, and counselor, took Joe and me on a visit to Deiheisha Camp to see the students again. Joe had just returned from New York, where he attended his mother's funeral. We had visited Deiheisha two months before. We have over 120 students there. The sewage rivulets along the paths are still there, houses piled together on the hillside, each an ugly growth of cement rooms, small dusty yards, rusty iron beams, tiny iron-framed windows. The Israeli radio, celebrating the 40th anniversary, simply declared that the West Bank was quiet during the celebration. Widespread curfews, particularly in the camps, had facilitated the peaceful celebrations. Perhaps they have taken Kissinger's 'off the record' advice to heart, 'Seal it and crush it.' That's precisely what happened to Deiheisha during the week of curfew. 'The worst since '67' was the repeated phrase. Sealed, cut off from the press, the place was saturated with troops. Specialists at terror were brought in by helicopter. Two days after the curfew had ended, we saw enough to make us quite sick. Everywhere, windows were smashed, houses raided, and what furniture and home objects they had were wrecked. Beatings, raids, and arrests were continuous. A father broke the curfew in desperation to get food for his family. He was caught and asked whether he wanted his leg or arm broken. Young boys were dragged from their homes and beaten. Joe and I insisted on seeing one. Our students took us to a home where a young teenager had an arm in plaster, and his elder brother a shoulder healing from gunshot wound. We visited many homes. I was delighted to have around me, at one point, five of my students, to whom I taught intensive English three years ago. They soon slipped away as signals were passed from alley to alley that troops were close. We carry our passports on these visits. You do not generally see young men in the camps. Small five-year olds you do see, running down the paths, carrying small Palestinian flags, acting out what their impressionable minds have witnessed during the previous days. We left Deiheisha after four hours, weary and deeply troubled. Frustrated too, as I suppose so many people are when they see deep injustice and desperate to communicate it to the decision-makers who could influence the course of events. The sun still shines on Summit Avenue.

As I travel to Seattle University to resume my studies there, I realize how everyone you meet is caught up in his own environment and concerns. Visiting Second Street in New York made me aware of the problems confronting American society in the centre of cities. I have vivid pictures of the homeless, curled up asleep on the subway that rides down to the splendour of the World Trade Centre, or the down-and-outs sleeping on the side-walks, smelling of their own excrement and sweat, or the night noise in the streets below, where young blades, cursing and fighting, disturb one's sleep with their verbal battles. Or in St. Paul, where Michael Lee Anderson runs the Christian Brothers Youth Home for boys who are unable to stay with their families; or for Bob Walsh, involved in the Guadalupe Area Project for dropouts in the same city.

The Uprising or, as I prefer to call it, the 'explosion' has entered every facet of life in the occupied territories of the West Bank. Joe and I drove south, as we had weeks before, to villages where our students lived. Beit Ummar was the village we visited. We tried to see as many as we could of the twenty-five students we have there. This beautiful, peaceful village, even though partially cleaned up, still had in its main street the appearance of a town suffering a minor earthquake. Two hundred troops and two bulldozers had ripped through the centre of the village. The machines widened the road on both sides, taking down sides and frontages of houses, steps, verandas, balconies, gardens, orchards, walls, gates, wrecking shops, destroying factory machinery, damaging cars and tractors beyond repair. The mosque, the pride of this rural religious people, stood shattered, not a pane of glass remaining. The people sat in the dust rubble, still dazed and in a state of disbelief.

The staff in the Bethlehem University were constantly inquiring after information about students. From various sources we began to list names, particularly of students in prison. When I left, I had a list of over thirty. I suspect the list represents only a small proportion of the total. Of those we know, one girl was sentenced to 25 years imprisonment, another young man to 21 years, and many without being brought to court for six months, and a larger number for unspecified periods. Eventually news came from Maria Homburg, dean of nursing, who visits the hospitals where most of our student nurses are working voluntarily, that a woman student Maysoun, was in Bethlehem hospital. Visits to her opened our eyes to the results of shootings and beatings. We saw an example of gunshot wounds on a young man from Gaza. The bullet travelled through his stomach and into his spine, destroying the spinal column. Later, we heard that over twenty injured were brought from Deiheisha, including students of ours. One particular case upset me especially—that of a young woman married a few months back and in her third year at the University, shot in the back with a rubber bullet, resulting in her aborting a three-month fetus. When I left Bethlehem, Anton, Joe and Austin were daily helping at a rehabilitation centre."

It was during my stay in the United States that I was given a copy of David Grossman's "The Yellow Wind." This remarkable book, in which there was a chapter devoted to Bethlehem University, describes James Connolly, my fellow walker around the environs of the Bethlehem area. He was delighted about "his blue-eyed, British sly smile." I recollect, also, just missing Ted Koppel, on TV Channel 7 devoting an entire week to the situation on the West Bank and Israel. All is not lost because there are many sensitive and gifted Israelis and Jews.

It was faces of Palestinians that stayed in my memory even when travelling across the vastness of North America. Both David Grossman and I'm sure Ted Koppel were seeking for the truth. I ended my writing with: "And so too, truth and beauty remain for those who seek them. I can hardly forget how Maysoun's face, as she suffered in her hospital bed, transformed into the inimitable Palestinian smile of delight and pleasure when I told her we went to see her home and family in Bani Na'im. Did you see my home? Isn't it wonderful? And the flowers, my garden, the beautiful flowers!"

XIV / KITES ARE FLYING HIGH OVER BETHLEHEM

Kites are flying high up above Manger Square and the roofs of Bethlehem. Thermals drive them hundreds of feet up with their colourful streamers straining against the hazy blue sky and the pink glow on the desert hills in the sinking western sun. I chuckled to myself. Three years ago when I was appointed campus minister at Bethlehem University I presented to the Vice-Chancellor suggestions for community activities for the students. One idea was a kite festival. It drew an impatient and rather angry response, almost scorn. "You'll have the military up here within minutes!" How ironic that during the Intifada dozens of young and not so young Palestinians are enjoying this relaxing activity.

I arrived back on the first Sunday in September and walked down in the late afternoon for 5:30 Mass at the Franciscans' Parish in Manger Square. After my work in United States and visit to England I was reminded immediately of the sadness of the whole situation here. The streets and alleyways that wind down through Bethlehem near the market were empty. The place seemed dead with rubbish and rubble strewn everywhere. As I entered the square a group of Christian Palestinians left the Nativity Church melting quietly away to their home at the end of a wedding: how unlike the noise, colour and cavalcade of previous times! In front of the police station twenty or so Israeli reservists stood, lolled or sat on their jeeps probably thoroughly bored and thinking of their homes and families. The square was free of traffic and the shops were closed. I felt, momentarily, a pang of home sickness for the rich rural green intimacy of the high hedgerows near Shaftesbury and the bustle of Bromley Market Square: places where my family live.

I discovered that the shops open only between 9:00–12:00 noon during the week. I met students in the streets as I walked through Bethlehem. Of the young men I met over one third of them had been in prison, some of them twice and for as long as six months. Apparently at the present time the university community has well over a hundred in prison, three shot dead, several seriously injured and one member of staff imprisoned for six months, another, now released, for eighteen days and many staff members called in for interrogation. Some measure of the extent of arrests can be gauged when it is considered that Bethlehem University is a small institution of 1500 students and 140 staff.

With two Sisters of St. Joseph on the Bethlehem University staff I visited Deiheisha Camp. All was quiet as a young man shot with a dum dum bullet two weeks before, lay dying with gangrene in his stomach in hospital. The people in the camp did not want to cause disturbances so as to avoid a curfew which would prevent them attending the expected funeral. It was interesting visiting one house in the camp to see a mother's anxiety when troops arrived nearby and her sons went to the door of the house. She physically intervened and literally threw them back into the room. Neither young men had experienced detention during the Intifada.

During the time I was away groups of staff continued the pastoral outreach to the villages. With the help of the U.N. we were able to visit Gaza where we have over fifty students. I spent one afternoon seeing students in the village of Halhul that lies on the hills either side of the Hebron road, thirty minutes by road south of Bethlehem. It was a delight to meet so many young people. Inspite of all their suffering they still have the laughter and welcome so typical of them. We talked about the large number of students that have married during the Intifada. Various theories were put forward, one of which was the claim that marriage expenses were considerably less since there were no celebrations.

Yousif Al-Hreimi was a particular example of a student friend of mine who I kept in contact with and whose character I found exceptional. I used to visit him occasionally. Why was he so special and important?

To start with, he had presence. He was always—as far as I recalled—gentle and calm. Could this young, fervent, Moslem of twenty-two years have discovered already how to grasp life's vicissitudes and encapsulate them with a philosophy, a set of values, and a deep faith in God that brings such equanimity?

With this presence was his continuing graciousness, I cast my mind back to Newmans's idea of a gentleman and I cannot help but place Yousif into the Cardinal's description. There was about him a genuine courtesy which, because it is sincere, you do not expect to be shallow or motivated by secondary considerations.

All the more remarkable is the consistency of his behaviour, which for lesser mortals, would have erupted in self pity or anger, at the suffering and hardships he endured. For over a year he made light of a severe, painful kidney complaint. He kept quiet about the death of his father who had just died from cancer. He did not fret, as many can do, about his new responsibilities and financial straits of his extended family. Nor did he volunteer to tell me that both his brothers were in prison. I had to find out. Quite calmly and in a business-like way he would come to my office with his friends to talk about the lessons during office hours. I would ask how he was getting on. He would say clearly if he had difficulties and would quietly suggest improvements in the lessons. I liked his friends too. What a really fine group of people! They offered genuine friendship, not claiming a return. I felt comfortable and good about it all.

I first met Yousif near his house, which is situated below a road that circles round the back of Bethlehem. I was struggling, unsuccessfully to capture in water colours, in the afternoon light and shadow, the ziggurat-like mass of housing that clung to the south-east slopes of the town. His house was on the top side of a valley on a small terrace. It was a small dwelling. If I recall correctly, there were some sheep, pigeons or doves, a small plot of crops. All was rather simple but well ordered.

He came with another Moslem student on one of my walking outings east of the Herodian. There were nearly a hundred staff and their families, secretaries, and students all loaded up with Arabic food for a good picnic near the caves. Issa had come, not thinking he would need lunch. I managed and quite readily collected food for them. They were most polite but said they, as strict Moslems, could not eat the meat I gave them.

By now you may have considered him to be rather a pretentious individual. I didn't find him that way. He had a great sense of humour, joined in lessons in a fairly vigorous manner and was honest about the opinions he held. When the Moslem Brotherhood was placing pressure on the University administration for a Mosque, he was one of the forty or so, on Friday, who prayed outside the Brothers' residence front door. The rows of prostrate bodies made it difficult to get into the house to take the customary light lunch. When this was happening, I recollect clearly, the crowd of Christian students—was it fear or indignation—that pressed them into the University chapel for midday Mass that Friday?

Why is he, for me, one of the faces of the Intifada? I think he is, because he represents some of the contradictions; his attitudes and behaviour demonstrate how remarkable "goodness" can be when surrounded by evil and violence. I want to return to the evening when the troops came to destroy his home. The sequence of events described by him, blow by blow, and his final response at the end of it all is what I would dearly see more of amongst all the hatred and fear on the part of Israelis and Palestinians.

He told me he was watching television late in the evening. He had, as was his custom, finished his prayers. Suddenly, he heard a loud series of noises. Perhaps, he said, it was local youths starting a night demonstration: something not uncommon in his part of Bethlehem. He went outside his house expecting to see soldiers confronting young men who had assembled a stone barricade. His house was just below the road. When he looked up all he saw were the boots of a large group of soldiers above him. He was fearful since he thought they might arrest him. After all, numerous arrests were made at night during the Intifada. His mother was already asleep, he was tempted to hide in the toilet, he dreaded the idea of prison. On returning to the house, however, he found soldiers already inside. They had awoken his mother and seeing him they asked "Where is Ibrahim?" "Is he at home?" His seventeen year old brother was already in prison arrested three months before and detained in the "Moskoubyeh" prison, a place of harsh treatment and torture near Jerusalem. "Who are you? Give me your papers!" Shouted the officer. When it was realized he was Ibrahim's brother, the officer thrust the official order at him declaring the intention to blow up the house. "You have twenty minutes to clear the house" he snapped.

He realized, then, that the military were going to destroy his home as a result of the accusation made against his young brother who was in prison. He was in prison without any official accusation or trial and his six month administrative detention could be renewed, Yousif told me that the lawyer had only been to see him once and on that occasion his brother had not admitted to throwing the molotov cocktail inspite of repeated interrogations.

Blowing up of houses on the West Bank and Gaza is nothing new. According to Yousif over fifteen hundred homes have been destroyed since 1967 and sixty percent of this total during the Intifada. He said the house for a Palestinian represented something quite sacred. His home held in his mind a long family history of memories, traditions and people; to see it destroyed in a few seconds with dynamite was a crushing blow. He never thought the military would do this in Bethlehem, which was a place where tourists and pilgrimages came daily from all over the world. The soldiers came at night, he said, like thieves, they broke in suddenly, for the occupying army worked at all hours.

Apparently five soldiers were in the house and a dozen stood guard outside. The officer told him to hurry, he only had twenty minutes. Yousif replied that it was impossible to remove all the furniture unless he was given time to get help from his neighbours.

"No, this is a military zone. Nobody is allowed in or out. The soldiers will give you a hand." A military zone can be declared anywhere at any time putting absolute restrictions and controls upon those who live within it.

So everything was thrown outside in haste. The refrigerator, sacks of rice, sugar, in such a way that they would never be used again. Meanwhile his grand parents still slept; they were heavy sleepers and had not heard the noise. He had almost forgotten them in their room. He dreaded the moment facing them after all their recent sufferings with the loss of their son, their grandsons in prison, and now the very roof over their heads was to be destroyed.

The soldiers continued their work as though it was a routine. "Do you find this human?" Yousif asked one of them. "Do you think this is just, you who claim to come from a democratic state?" The young Israeli answered: "No, I don't think it just. But these are the orders!"

Yousif then took the animals out of the area near the house. He had looked after them since his brother Omar, who dreamed of being a veterinary surgeon, was taken to prison in a centre called "Ansar 3" in the Negev. The name "Ansar 3" was given to this new prison during the Intifada after the sinister prison camp that existed when the Israeli army entered Lebanon. Yousif said he did not have time to remove the bird cages or the eggs, these were destroyed in the explosion. The pigeons did escape and later in the day continued to fly distractedly over the ruins of their home. One of the soldiers beat a weak young lamb which was amongst the sheep. Yousif asked him why he beat the creature. The only response he received was: "You fuck off, or I'll hit you also!"

Later, a soldier asked him for twenty nails, he realized afterwards that they were needed to fix the dynamite. The explosion was extremely powerful. After the demolition a cloud of smoke and ash floated in the air for five minutes. Yousif's mother wept and cried out invoking God. Such was the force of the explosion that neighbouring houses were damaged. The officer used a strong torch to see if the work was complete. The soldiers then left.

For several days they lived in tents beside the ruins of their house. Tents, apparently, are illegal under the occupation, but the Red Cross supplied them nonetheless Yousif's grand parents went to live in his uncle's house because they could not cope with the conditions.

Yousif explained to me in his unobtrusive way that he would never forget that night. The tears will not leave his eyes. Yet, he told me, the night had changed him. He would give his life to the search for peace in his land. He hoped he would be given the energy and strength to realize what he thought was his mission in life.

When I reflect on his words, I am quite astounded. I believe in his sincerity and good intent. His attitude gives us hope in a land where individuals on both sides hold ferociously to extreme views. Yet whilst he held these extraordinary views the Uprising continues.

Further disorder and anarchy has spread with the regretable disunity amongst some of the Palestinians. The HAMAS, the Islamic extremists, are battling for control with the Intifada.

Strike days ordered by the Intifada are challenged by the Hamas who force other strikes on the population. I, with another Brother, was returning from Manger Square up the steps near the Syrian Church at 11:30 A.M., on a Saturday, half an hour before the shops closed, when a youth, his head covered in a kaffiyeh threw bottles at us from five yards away: not a pleasant experience really. As we entered the passageway shots were fired from the direction of the Salesian

Technical School. Another young man, ironically the leader of the Moslem brothers at the University, grabbed me and pulled me into his shop until it quieted down. Troops were everywhere and the usual signs of a running battle were evident. By the Star Hotel, the leader of a section of reservists, a quietly spoken man in his early forties, perhaps an accountant or clerical worker, was obviously under stress and probably fairly frightened. He was distracted by the owner of the hotel who claimed bullets had smashed his car window. Stone barricades blocked the Frères Street to the University, the soldier said his men would not harm us but did not guarantee what was around the corner. Earlier, another Brother was hit by a fairly large stone on his shoulders as he returned from working with the injured young men in the rehabilitation centre.

I suppose I search for human faces behind these awful problems. It was Yousif who told me that the soldiers who destroyed his house came next day in some sympathy; it was soldiers who helped change the tyre of our Arab registered Peugeot car near Tantur, it was soldiers who offered our Vice-Chancellor water in the blazing heat when he cycles to Jerusalem. Good and evil exists on both sides in this fast moving, unpredictable land. The difficulties in finding a solution to the problems are immense as Landrum Bolling, the retiring principal, pointed out in his last lectures at Tantur. But for my students, young and intelligent, all they have known is occupation over the last twenty-one years. They see, on the West Bank alone, over fifty percent of the land and seventy percent of the available annual water supply directly controlled and used by the Israelis and settlers. They see their freedom and lives strangled by a creeping and now virtually complete annexation.

Playing with kites reminds me of Coventry Patmore's poem "Toys." I used to fit into the syllabus for Victorian Literature, amongst the major poets, less known favourites of mine. Francis Thompson's, "Hound of Heaven," was an example; "Toys" by Patmore another.

In "Toys" a father punishes his small son and dismisses him. He relents and visits him in his bedroom. He sees "on a table drawn beside his head" his son's most cherished toys that "comfort his sad heart." That night the Father wept and prayed to God

"Ah, when at last we lie with tranced breath,
Not vexing Thee in death,
And Thou rememberest of what toys we made our joys."

In Beit Jala the other afternoon a little boy was hurriedly constructing a kite probably working eagerly to sail it in the late afternoon thermals. It seems that each evening more kites reach upwards their silhouettes against the sky.

XV / "THERE IS AN APPOINTED TIME FOR EVERYTHING"

According to the words of wisdom based on an Hellenistic philosophy, life is a circle going round and round. It is now well into October 1988. The University has been closed for almost a year; the Intifada has raged for eleven months; the cycle of events associated with the Uprising will soon complete a full year.

It was after dinner, just a few evenings ago in our university residence, I was chatting with one of our guests over coffee. Quite inadvertently she started talking about herself, something she does not do very often. As she talked it struck me forcefully how her life revealed a cycle of experiences which were, in some sense, repeated with a profound sense of irony.

I first meet Miss Bie in one of the several small offices in the University Finance Department. She is a short woman in her sixties, someone you would not really notice in a crowd. She does not stand out at first mainly because she is discreet, quietly efficient in her administrative post, assisting Sister Miriam, who is the Financial Vice-President of the University. Her native tongue is French and she is most endearing when she speaks English in a very French sort of way.

She was born in 1926 in a village called Rixensart, not far from Brussels, into a very Christian family of four girls. They suffered the hardships of the 1930's depression. Her father, an entrepreneur in the building trade, lost almost everything once the economy virtually collapsed. She became very active in various Catholic organizations when she went to school. Before the Second World War she befriended a young Jewish girl at school. The Jewish girl attended the classes and they became companions. Miss Bie said that after Belgium was overrun the girl used to wear the yellow star, but tried to hide it most of the time. She recalls also, taking her for a weekend outing picnicking in the countryside. The following Monday the Jewish girl was not in class. She never saw her again.

During the German occupation 1940-1945, though she was not involved with the resistance, she was indirectly, but she did not always realize it; she used for example to carry messages from house to house. A small fourteen year old girl carrying a case would not be noticed. Towards the end of the war whilst Belgium was still occupied, when she was a young woman and eighteen years old, she joined a group of several young people led by a Jesuit priest who helped rescue children who were victims of the heavy bombing. They acquired, through the Red Cross, a truck and had permission to drive round collecting homeless children and then look after them in accommodations they arranged.

It was at this time that the Red Cross approached them saying they were desperately trying to save several hundred Jewish children. Could they hide and look after sixty of them. They took over an unused cinema and stayed with the children for two weeks. Some of the children came from Germany and had thus far survived the Holocaust. They were (boys and girls) aged from three to fifteen years old. When the children arrived, she was somewhat embarrassed as to how they were all going to live in the one open cinema hall with only one toilet. Miss Bie was amazed, how the older children led and organized. That evening the girls were changing behind curtains, beds were segregated and plenty of common sense and initiative displayed. She also admired, even under these severe conditions when at any moment they could be discovered— incidently the Gestapo offices were just across the street opposite the cinema— the Jewish children attempted to maintain their customs of eating, and praying. The Red Cross came at night with food. Apparently, she said, the Gestapo were suspicious and were very close to finding out what was going on. During that time, however, furious fighting had developed between the Germans and the resistance, the bombing had increased and the British and American armies were close. The liberation of Brussels saved them; she calculated another ten days would have made their position impossible. However, the children then dipersed to various Jewish families and agencies. She often wonders where they are now.

Directly after the war Miss Bie joined a new lay institute known as the "Association Fraternelle Internationale" and in the United States as the Inter Cultural Association. She intended going abroad on the missions, but spent sixteen years in administration and training young candidates for their association. The whole structure of her group changed in the late 1960's and she volunteered to work in the Holy Land in 1969. She ran with her close friend, Sister Patricia of the St. Joseph order, a hostel for Israeli Arabs who were just beginning to attend the Hebrew University. This was her first contact with Arabs and the Arab-Israeli problems. The hostel was a great success, but came under criticism for its liberal and forward-looking policies. By 1981, both Miss Bie and Sister Patricia were dismissed. Miss Bie felt a keen sense of injustice. She was prepared to leave and return to Europe. She told me that on Easter Sunday she attended Mass at the Greek Catholic Church in the Old City. Monsignor Lutfi, during his sermon, thanked the pilgrims for coming to pray with the

Palestinian Christians and asked them to pray that the Arabs would have the strength to stay in the Holy Land. This made Miss Bie realize that for years she had told her students the same thing. She decided to stay.

Brother Joe, the Vice-Chancellor of Bethlehem University offered her a post looking after the book store. Later she worked for a short time in a home for the blind. She always had that desire to work in pastoral areas as well as administration. She also felt that the book store post at the Bethlehem University could be quite adequately staffed by a Palestinian. However, the blind home work did not last, and she returned to Bethlehem University where she now works in the finance department.

How did she feel as an expatriate during these unpredictable times of the uprising? She always believed that the Arabs had been treated unjustly and she saw the Intifada was an opportunity for the Palestinians to take the situation into their own hands. As someone who had suffered an occupation for five years and had seen the well-organized resistance in Belgium she had wondered during the twenty years of Israeli occupation on the West Bank and Gaza, why the Arabs were not apparently better organized. She was quick to identify the Intifada as something different and understood the feelings and attitudes, particularly of the young people.

Nevertheless, she was afraid of the price the people were having to pay for the protests they made and the increasingly harsher responses of the Israeli Military Government. At the same time she suffered the mounting frustration of wanting to help and be involved, experiencing and seeing all the suffering going on around her. She recognized that the Palestinians wanted to do things themselves and she had to be a convinced bystander. By her presence, her availability to work in the finance department and the discreet use of her small salary, she continues to help others.

Somewhere, Teilhard de Chardin wrote (in a beautiful passage) "God must, in some way or other, make room for himself, hollowing us out and emptying us, if He is finally to penetrate into us." I feel with Miss Bie's life of devotedness, giving and often suffering, this transformation is taking place. There is a centre to her being which is unshakeable and quite fearless. She has remarkable ability to perceive things as they are, to recognize their inner reality and then to accept them in faith in a peaceful and positive way.

My experience listening to Miss Bie and the impact of events that continue to unfold around me found a bitter sense of irony in the cycle of readings for daily Mass which came recently from Ecclesiastes:

"There is a time to plant and a time to uproot the plant.
A time to kill, and time to heal."

October is the season to gather the olive harvest. This year the olives are plentiful and the harvest is being picked unusually early. In Bethlehem the olive press is situated in an unpretentious large room opening out onto the pavement of the steep hill that enters Manger Square. This year, apparently, it may not open. Sadly the occupying military power will grasp at this vital seasonal ritual, in order to control, to impose more taxes and to harass the indigenous population. Already much of the grape harvest, now almost finished, lies rotting, the growers unable to export their produce and livelihood to their customary markets. In the hills north of Hebron the fruit trees, such as those with the vast plum harvest in Beit Ummar, are left unpicked partly because the troops prevent the villagers from picking the fruit and also because the military governor has forbidden the growers to market their produce. These good hill farming people rely so much on their horticultural living to survive; it will be a hard winter.

Restrictions continue to control the attempts to educate the young people on the West Bank. Colleagues of mine, principals of schools in the Bethlehem region, were summoned to the Military Governor at a few hours' notice on the fifteenth of September. They were told, for security reasons, no classes would be opened in the foreseeable future. Secondly, that teaching any child, at any time and in any place would incur heavy punishment. The earlier efforts to run schooling in peoples' homes was crushed and some of those responsible imprisoned without trial for six months. The announcement, made earlier, that schools would open at the beginning of October proved to be a false promise just as more recently the statement that schools and Universities may open in mid-November. I noted in the American Assistant Secretary of State Murphy's address to the B'nai B'rith convention in Baltimore, that "the closing of institutions in the occupied territories, particularly schools, has not ended the violence."

Regardless of the closure of all schools since early February, violence certainly continues unabated. During a two week period, for example, between 28th August and 10th September, on the West Bank and Gaza Strip, twenty-eight villages, camps and towns have suffered curfews. Without counting the continous night curfews in the Gaza Strip there were no fewer than a hundred days curfew in these locations. Meanwhile the death toll, according to Palestinian sources reaches over 330 people and the numbers of demonstrations multiplied.

The words of Ecclesiastes again serves as a counterpoint in our daily life; there is:

"A time to scatter stones, and a time to gather them.
A time for love and a time to hate."

Peter, an American Jesuit priest on the staff of the University was returning home at 9:00 p.m., after visiting a community in Bethlehem when a jeep came up behind him. He was ordered, in the dark and at gun point, to pick up stones. There were a few small barriers of stones at the corner of Frères Street. What he did not realize, and perhaps the soldiers too, that around the corner were a series of stone obstructions, row upon row, arranged with mathematical precision. The soldiers ordered a Palestinian man from a neighbouring house to assist. He complained saying he would lose face appearing in the street in his pyjamas. It took them close to half an hour to clear the road. All the small roads around us are frequently blocked to prevent jeeps chasing groups of youths that almost daily battle in the precincts of Bethlehem at around midday and then retreat, very often, into our neighbourhood. Just this Saturday, October 1st, three young men were shot. One of them was hit in the chest while standing just outside the photographer's shop. Little boys and girls later heaped small stones covering the pool of his blood that remained on the road way.

Some of the results of this kind of shooting I see when I spend time each morning helping in the rehabilitation centre in Bethlehem. Six members of the Brothers community help in various ways, most of us with basic physiotherapy. There are twelve young Palestinians struggling to recover. One young man has eight bullet wounds and as he lay wounded saw his mother, father and two brothers shot dead. Three of the injured are paralysed, all of them paraplegics. We discovered today that one of them found out his mother had died a few days before. The news failed to reach him owing to the sealing off of the Hebron area. He has a temperature of 103 degrees Fahrenheit and suffers an infection in his urinary tract. The Israeli defence minister, Yitzak Rabin was reported in the "Jerusalem Post" saying he was "not worried" by the sharp rise in casualties among the participants in violent protests, declaring "this is precisely our aim." I sometimes wonder about man's inhumanity to man.

Arrests and imprisonment without trial continue and it would appear that all forms of leadership are suspect. For example, John and I on one of our afternoon walks, which we sometimes call "mashi mashi" in our limited Arabic, came close to witnessing this. Returning downhill in the side streets of Beit Jala a Palestinian shouted from a window. He was a brother of one of the University staff. "Do go to see Jehad, he has to report to the military tomorrow; we fear he will be arrested." We wended our way past the Greek Orthodox Church that stands prominently on the brow of the hill through narrow streets and eventually found his house. In his quiet way he was so glad to see us, particularly John who was a friend of his family. We sat in the kitchen around the table. On the table were rows of University library books. Jehad is a voracious reader. The books, he said gently, will need returning to the library. Calmly he asked us both to return other books to various individuals. He said he would be arrested the following day. He was concerned for his wife who was visiting her family in Russia and would be returning soon. It was quite uncanny sipping a soft drink and listening to this man in his thirties, a scholar and a fairly unobtrusive personality, wearing heavy spectacles and smoking his customary cigarette from the corner of his mouth. In his quiet and orderly way he was preparing for his departure with a sense of inevitability. We left him saying we would think of him and pray for him. I don't think he was a religious man, but the promise of prayers and our concern seemed to reassure him. Next day we heard that he set off for the military with a small case with his clothes in it. He did not return. He is in prison near Hebron and will probably be there for six months.

The Palestinian people I meet remain determined about their identity and their rights. Inevitably they have moments of despondency realizing their present reality and comparing it with their aspirations and ideals. Khaled stood outside, his hands grasping the tall iron railings that encircle the campus. I had known him for over three years. He was depressed, and wanted to get on and make something of his life. He had just lost his job on a building site in Israel. The employer sacked him because he did not appear on strike days. How could he? Leaving Deiheisha for work on a strike day would result in the firing of his home.

His home was two rooms in the centre of the camp. His hope of completing his education was delayed by the closure of the University for almost a year. He wanted desperately to get out of the refugee camp, to buy some land and build a home in fresh air, space and freedom. He was in love, he told me. He had seen her father but she was beautiful and other men wanted her too. A few days later he introduced me to Iman. There she stood smiling in her long grey Arab dress and white head scarf. She could only be fifteen. She was beautiful too, beautiful in a distinctive Palestinian way. "She is in second secondary," he said. "I will wait and marry her after she has finished her education." I could only say to myself, "Oh, I do hope so! I do hope so!"

Volleys of gunfire rattled up the valley slopes below us. A split second after one retort an agonzied yell was heard from a group of young men behind the walls. Someone was hit. On the following Sunday morning all was quiet and it was then that I noticed two very large Palestinian flags flying in the morning breeze on the top of a tall cyprus tree. Although the area had been saturated with troops some young bravados had perilously climbed the tree at night and placed a pole with the flags attached. Groups of people appeared on their flat roofs and verandas looking across the valley at the flags. In the pale early sun there appeared traces of pride and pleasure on their morning faces.

Alistaire Cook, on the Sunday B.B.C. World Service, reminds us of a larger world. Both the American and the Israeli elections are close at hand. I'm intrigued how he skilfully weaves his web and in his pleasing cadences as he parallels present American baseball, with English cricket between the wars as foci of nations' interest. Vice-President Bush, apparently, was skilfully using baseball as an analogy in his campaign. Would that these elections could bring forth statesmen to meet the challenges around us! The radio announced Israeli soldiers were blown up in the buffer zone of Lebanon. How sad and terrible. And outside my room I hear the sharp cracks of automatic fire not far away. It's a daily occurence; I do not even to go the window. The Intifada is now a way of life.

XVI / DECLARATIONS AND ELECTIONS

The T-shirts worn by some tourists in the Holy Land are boldly inscribed with, "I got stoned during the Intifada". It was not quite clear to me whether the idea was their initiative or some sharp entrepreneurial operator in West Jerusalem. Whatever the case, the pun would, I think, be lost to a non-native speaker of English and certainly not be appreciated by the suffering Palestinians who see the struggle continuing unabated for a long time to come. The election results in Israel and America and responses to the declaration of a State of Palestine were not too encouraging for them.

This struggle intensified particularly during the week of the elections and the PLO meeting in Algiers. Bethlehem had not, to my knowledge, experienced the full rigours of a military curfew during the Uprising. Hundreds of days of curfews during the Intifada were imposed on refugee camps, villages and towns like Nablus, Jenin, Tulkarem, but not Bethlehem. Close by, we had seen the camps in and near Bethlehem and particularly the town of Beit Sahour endure curfews during November, 1988. Our turn came on Tuesday 15th November when the Palestinian National Council meeting in Algiers was expected to declare a Palestinian State. In order to prevent demonstrations and celebrations, the whole of the West Bank and Gaza were sealed off and declared a closed military zone.

At about 3:30 a.m. on Tuesday 15th November I awoke from my sleep disturbed by the crackle and blare of loudspeakers. Army jeeps with powerful speakers drove around the dark empty streets of Bethlehem announcing that a curfew was imposed by the Military Governor until further notice. The inhabitants listened from their beds to the repeated broadcasts which continued until about 6:30 a.m. They were told that no one was to leave their homes and if they did so, they would seriously endanger themselves. From my window, I saw bright intense search lights panning the walls and windows of buildings as the military motored around.

The day proved to be a strange experience in an atmosphere of complete stillness, the town appeared deserted. Nothing moved anywhere except for the occasional military jeep or truck making that familiar droning noise with its heavy army tyres on the roads. Just before 9:00 a.m. an Arab car appeared from a side street, the occupant must have been a heavy sleeper and not heard the curfew announcement. Like an angry bee a jeep appeared immediately. And similar to a scene in Keystone Cops, the soldiers gave chase towards Rachel's Tomb, intercepting the car as it negotiated the roundabout. It seemed that any noise or movement only served to enhance the eerie silence in the warm sunny morning.

Later in the day some families discreetly appeared on their flat roofs and verandas. There were no Palestininan flags. Apparently the latest military directive made flag flying a five year prison sentence. One sharp observer, however, pointed out to me the arrangement and colours of items of washing as they hung on lines to dry in the sun. On some of the washing lines red, white, green and black colours were clearly visible: the Palestinian colours!

As evening darkness fell, military vehicles drove down streets with search lights. It was a most weird scene. Powerful beams of light scanned the town. Some of the beams were so powerful, they gave the impression of intense lasers cutting across Bethlehem. Suddenly from the darkness a mosque minaret, then towers of various churches, St. Catherines, the Nativity, the Greek Catholic, the Salesians, would light up sharp white projected against the black sky. As troops approached, local youths pierced the night air with loud whistles to warn people of the soldiers' proximity. At one moment, our hillside simply echoed with this shrill cacophony. Whilst this unrehearsed and extaordinary "son et lumiere" of Bethlehem was enacted before our privileged hill top position, occasional fireworks went off. Mischievous, clandestine splutters of golden or bright white fountains sparkled as the whiz of a small rocket tracing its parabola, burst and then disappeared. It was enough to send into action even more mobile troops attempting to identify the offenders. There were, as far as I know, no processions or demonstrations so tight was the control. Nevertheless, families celebrated quietly in their homes.

Typical of these spontaneous celebrations was the experience of Ibtissan and her friends. On the evening of the curfew she was in her father-in-law's house with four friends. They were listening to radio Monte Carlo. During a news bulletin an announcement was made asking all Palestinians to go to their roofs and balconies and celebrate the declaration of a Palestinian State with fireworks.

In the enthusiasm of the moment, and forgetting the curfew, they went out on to the balcony. From their house on the high slopes of Bethlehem they saw numerous fireworks gleaming in the night down in Beit Sahour. Not to be outdone they brought wire wool—the pads used to clean the sauce pans in the kitchen—and made sparklers of the material.

They must have been quite jolly and this attracted the attention of the troops. Within seconds a loud crash shook them and rubber bullets splattered around the balcony. The shouting and the noise of soldiers' heavy boots on the road below sent them rushing indoors. Moments later the metal front door shuddered with heavy blows from the soldiers. The young women and men were frozen with fear. Ibtissan's father-in-law shouted back at the soldiers as they demanded entry into the house and smashed the windows on the ground floor. "Where are the women with the fireworks?" The father-in-law said he did not know what they were talking about and told them they must come around the side of the house since the door they were beating was not in use.

Like many Palestininan extended families they often have several houses quite close together. Ibtissan and her companions fled from her father-in-law's house across a small courtyard into one of the other houses belonging to the family.

The young men hid in a cupboard and the young women huddled together crying, almost hysterical, in the back room. By now twelve troops were arguing with Ibtissan's father-in-law. Ibtissan feared for her father-in-law and said she was going to give herself up. The others refused to let her go persuading her she would be sent to prison. They also told her that there would be no one to look after her two young children.

Finally, after some very awkward moments, the troops left frustrated. Fireworks were going off in various parts of Bethlehem by now. It was becoming too much like a game of Tom and Jerry for the weary soldiers. Whether the families celebrated in such an open manner with fireworks or not, one of my students explained to me that "all the armies in the world could not contain what she felt in her mind and heart."

The day before the curfew of Bethlehem witnessed the massive military build up. Returning in the dark in the early evening from Beit Jala I saw helicopters land on the secondary school playing fields. Troops stood guard on the roads and roof tops.

The helicopters' red, yellow and green lights flashed as the machines dipped and circled. On the Hebron Road heavy traffic moved with a certain urgency. Columns of military trucks, jeeps and other vehicles raced along with head lights on. The streets were saturated with foot patrols carrying ominous batons and wearing red berets; these were the real professionals. Hundreds of arrests were made and house to house searches undertaken in some areas. All telephones were cut for virtually a week. Road blocks prevented any Palestinian leaving the West Bank, and the following day most intersections had check points to prevent any movement during the curfew. The evening before the curfew, I went with one of my colleagues for our customary short evening constitutional after dinner. A jeep drew up beside us, a lamp shone in our faces, it was the military Governor's vehicle. Who were you? What were you doing? We explained. "Have a good day," came the courteous answer in English. "Well," I thought to myself, "under the circumstances, I'll try!"

There was no doubt what message the occupying military power wanted to achieve. Certainly for the last few days in Bethlehem, the army's presence was formidable. Nevertheless, President Chaim Herzog of Israel, when he opened the new Knesset, warned its newly elected members to avoid the mounting of anti Arab feeling. He said there were thirty-six injunctions in the Bible to respect the rights of minorities. He urged the Knesset to denounce attempts to whip up feeling against minorities and pointed out how the founding fathers of Israel "repeatedly emphasized that the state would be judged by its relationship with the Arabs".

It was just after the Palestinian National Conference in Algiers and the opening of the Knesset that I attended a symposium organized by The Foundation for Mideast Communication. The purpose of the meeting was to listen to two speakers, Daoud Kuttab, who was a journalist at the PNC in Algiers and Moshe Amirav, an Israeli politician, who sincerely seeks peace and justice with the Arabs.

The gathering took place in the pleasant dignified environment of the American Colony Hotel one evening on 28 November, 1988. Kuttab spoke first and explained how the PNC had not been reported accurately in both the world press and Israeli media. He said that at the conference there were significant new directions in both style and content in the PLO message.

In style, he argued, it was the first time at a PNC that decisions were made by a majority vote. Prior to this, decisions had to be unanimous, often reflecting the lowest common denominator. A further important change was the attitudes of the extreme minorities groups within the PLO. He cited the example of George Habash of the Popular Front for the Liberation of Palestine (PFLP), abdicating his position as the tyrannic minority. He was impressed by George Habash's speeches where he adopted a far more pragmatic approach realizing a just peace, from the Palestinian point of view, was impractical but a comprehensive peace should be the aim of all parties.

The change in content of the PLO message, particularly the Declaration, he thought, was even more significant. He recorded that the PLO now accepted UN resolution 181 and 242, did not mention the phrase "armed struggle," referred to the name Israel thirteen times in both positive and negative ways and used the word coexistence six times.

In history, he said, declaration statements of independence had not changed. If the Palestinian Declaration was true to history then, the conference had proclaimed: universal human rights, the set-up of a peace loving state, peaceful coexistence with its neighbours and the elimination of those things that generated fear between peoples. He said the Intifada had had a wide spread effect on the PLO decision-making process providing a new realistic moderate attitude. Mr. Kuttab further observed how the posture of the USSR had changed. Pressure from the USSR moderated the views of extremists.

Daoud Kuttab ended his address by pointing out some of the misreporting in the Israel press. Among the items distorted by the press was the timing of the Declaration. In the Israeli press it was reported that the delay in announcing the Declaration was to link it with the American TV networks, whereas the conference held back the news so that it coincided with the morning dawn prayers from the minarets in Palestine. He concluded that there was an ominous warning from the PLO. They wished to give moderation a chance; if it failed other approaches would be employed.

Moshe Amirav confirmed much of Kuttab's observations. He saw the PLO become increasingly more pragmatic and realistic rather than ideological. He did not see the Declaration as an explicit recognition of Israel. He saw both people caught in their own Catch-22 attitudes. The Israelis have the double message of experiencing unnecessary fear yet at the same time conscious of their great military power. Moshe Amirav confirmed his own experience here as a former member of the Likud party and a seasoned paratrooper in the 1967 war and in the invasion of Lebanon. For the Arabs, the double message lies in their wanting to see Israel disappear, yet at the same time recognizing the reality of their forceful presence. They now know that somehow they must compromise with reality.

Moshe Amirav pointed out that the PLO acceptance of UN 181 was more important than 242. The 181 resolution implies an economic confederation of states and the recognition of two different nations on one land. He said he left the Likud party because its ideas were impracticable and would lead to five more wars. Sensitivity and vision were needed for an inclusive decision for both Arabs and Jews.

Before I left the conference I had a short conversation with an Israeli man whose father left Russia to live in Wales, and where, so he explained, he was born. He had moved with his daughter to Israel eleven years ago. In answer to his question as to why I was in the Holy Land I explained I taught in Bethlehem University. "How's the teaching?" he asked. I explained we had been closed for a year and how the closure started with the demonstration and death of Isaac. "So you teach in houses then?" he asked hopefully. I explained the military government's order banning all teaching at any time and in any place. He was astonished. I liked him; we left each other shaking hands and saying "Shalom."

And so the liturgical year once again completes its cycle almost coinciding with the year of the uprising. Advent is about to start. With what hope we here will read and listen to the words: "Stir up thy might and come, O Lord," in what for me is the richest and most beautiful season in the church's calendar. Can the words of Isaiah be ever more poignant than now.

"He shall judge between nations" and
"They shall beat swords into plowshares
and their spears into pruning hooks."

I noticed too, the first reading in the liturgical hours St. Paul tells us:

"Do not stifle the spirit:
Do not despise prophecies.
Test everything; retain what is good."

Maybe my theme for Advent will be to continue to hope that the Declaration and the elections will bring eventually some solution to this troubled land.

XVII / THERE IS A PRICE TO PAY

The uprising has affected every facet of Palestinians lives. The cost in suffering is enormous. I would like to touch on some examples of the price paid by the ordinary people after one year of Intifada. Nouh, one of our older students who had been in prison some years ago, was deeply concerned about a friend of his, who had been in prison with him. His friend had just been taken off to prison again leaving his wife with two baby children without any support. There was no help from relations as most of them had left for Jordan. It was obvious that the stranded young wife and children, although they received some help from neighbours, would need assistance. Our student asked us for help. Brother Joe, the student and his wife eventually managed to reach Kalandia refugee camp which is to the north of Jerusalem. What they saw when they arrived was disturbing. The simple house was located on the periphery of the camp. It was built of rough crude concrete and had three small rooms and a tiny kitchen. The living room had four simple, stackable steel chairs, a cupboard that was virtually empty and no carpet on the concrete floor. In the bedroom there was no bed and the babies lay on mattresses close to the floor. The third small room had some goats which provided the only livelihood for the family; the husband was a shepherd. The kitchen, a tiny space, had an empty, small disconnected refrigerator. The house was draughty and very cold and damp. An electric fire was unused because the young mother could not pay for electricity. The visitors brought, on their second journey, six months supply of sugar, rice, oil and a supply of warm clothes from the Caritas Baby Hospital. They plan to go a third time with an oil heater and a supply of fuel. There must be many families in this type of predicament. Winter up in the hills is harsh and cold.

Though there are families who are suffering actually from the type of hardship mentioned above, many are not. Yet most families suffer from enormous stress, I take but one example which will, I hope, illustrate a wide ranging phenomenon.

Claudette and her husband and family live near Shepherds' Field. In fact their house has a splendid view of the pattern of fields with rich red-brown, alluvial soils, which over the centuries accumulated in the shallow valley east of the slopes of Bethlehem. From their veranda the red Dome and off-white stone work of the Greek Shepherds' Field church is only half a mile away across the gently sloping terrain. Also, the various spires and minarets of Beit Sahour and Bethlehem higher up on the ridge, stand out against the skyline, like clusters of stalagmites.

We have been friends of the family for years. Both my sisters visited them on their holiday in the Holy Land. Claudette and Michael are both highly educated people. Claudette speaks six languages, Michel three. Claudette is a teacher at a school in Bethlehem. Michel is a professional man. They married in 1971. She was sixteen and from a family in Bethlehem; Michel, at the time, penniless and having endured a life of extreme suffering, was born and educated in Beit Sahour. Michel was imprisoned in Jordan, Syria and Iraq. He had been highly political in his youth. He was smuggled out from Palestine into Syria. Whilst in prison he endured harsh conditions and was subject to torture. He later was trained professionally in Prague, and qualified in his specialization in London in 1982.

So Claudette is a wife of a very committed man. Her children, Marina who is now sixteen, Pauline thirteen and George eleven, are all bright and well educated. From my close association with this family I have seen the effects the Intifada has had on them, particularly the mother, who strives to hold them together when the accumulating stresses bring continuous and mounting tension.

Claudette explained that there were positive experiences with the Intifada. Beit Sahour, already a fairly tightly knit and often highly political community, has become more so during the Intifada. "People" she said, "related more with each other, felt more together." She thought the Palestinian problem was better understood worldwide with the press coverage. She was, as a mother, however, very concerned about her family. She rarely saw her husband. When he was not at his official work at the office, he was helping the people in Beit Sahour. Demonstrations were very often daily often daily occurrences. Both of them were heavily involved in the committees that unofficially organized their community. There were over thirty such cells in Beit Sahour to organize security, help with food supplies, those in need, crop growing and self-sufficiency schemes and of course at one time, education. Claudette, when the schools were closed, ran five classes in the rooms of neighbour's house.

As a mother, she was generally at home with the children. Most of the time there were enclosed. There was no schooling, and apart from a short period in the late summer, schools have been closed since before Christmas. She saw her bright children, bored, becoming unwilling to learn and picking up all the nuances, feelings and anger around them, They too were slowly and steadily becoming politicised. Often surrounded by troops, affected by the tear gas, which was regularly used, hearing and seeing the shooting, having troops invade and search the house, attitudes and even personalities were affected.

These stresses brought understandable friction and tension between husband and wife, between parents and children and between the children. There was no social life, few visits, no holidays, no celebration of Christmas, Easter or birthdays. They used to go into Jerusalem, holiday on the shores of the Lake of Galilee. All this appeared to be past and faded memories.

Stresses built up too, when George, having many of the traits of a fast-growing young boy, would disappear for hours. It was difficult to enforce disciplines in this situation. George would get involved in the demonstrations, perhaps put up flags, throw stones at soldiers. There was always the nightmare of receiving the news that he was killed or wounded or beaten or arrested. One of the tragedies of the present situation is certainly the damage done to the young people. In the legitimate protest about the gross injustices of the situation, the breakdown of the fabrics of the social order, inevitably effect the young. I see all around me young people in Bethlehem out of control. How they will ever settle down again to the discipline and commitment of school work is hard to gauge, "This is the price we must pay," say some. It does not alleviate the concern of parents, particularly mothers, who wish to see their children have a good life, to reach fulfillment and experience a good education.

Fear for the children is a mother's chief concern. Israeli responses to the demonstrations appear to vary. Claudette claimed that methods used in Beit Sahour, away from the eyes of tourists, were far harsher. She said tear gases were causing breathing problems, particularly if it entered the buildings. New bullets, which on impact leave a yellow liquid that inflames the skin, are used in Beit Sahour. Soldiers stop children in the street, stripping them to see if they have this yellow stain on their bodies. The troops have commandeered the school buildings in Beit Sahour for barracks, yet another sign of the determination of the Israelis to quell the Uprising.

Yet in spite of all this, I asked Claudette what her attitude toward the Jews was. She said she wished to live in harmony with them. She did not hate them, but she insisted that if they were to live together it should in equality, and that she should be recognized as a Palestinian. I asked her about her life as a Christian. She said she prayed more and this helped her to overcome her worries, She explained she prayed to Mary, Our Lady, especially.

So Claudette, for me, is the face of a mother, caring, protecting, nurturing her family in very difficult times. She says the Intifada had set the family back financially ten years. They have enough food as do most families, though I wonder how bad things will become this winter, if the uprising continues, particularly with the very poor families. She hopes for a future, but feels it will take a long, long time to achieve her aspirations. The way of life, rushing to the shops in the mornings, being locked up at home in the afternoons and evenings, experiencing curfews, unsure what each new day will bring, steadily seeing the attrition of their standard and quality of life eroded away, are things against which she must steel herself.

Families without food, families under stress suffer; but families with their entire homes destroyed are quite devastated materially and psychologically. Yesterday, I visited four homes that were destroyed by the military in the village of El-Khader.

"We're going to the village of El-Khader. Yesterday they destroyed four houses. Coming?" I had seen Issa's house some time after it had been destroyed, I had not witnessed the scene immediately after a detonation, "Yes," I said, "I'd like to come." We rushed off in a battered red Fiat, five of us, down the Hebron Road. Ten minutes later just before the bend where a road branches off to Solomon's Pools, we turned right under an archway entering the village of El-Khader. "The first house is just on the left," said our driver.

As we alighted from the car we saw a small crowd. A new and fairly large building containing shops on the ground floor and several apartments above, lay in a tangled heap of concrete, twisted steel wire and debris. We met the families that lived there, One of the young men was a graduate of ours. We awkwardly expressed our sympathy to the families. Apparently this house was destroyed by a bulldozer. An explosion would have damaged the houses close by.

The second house was destroyed by TNT. Twenty-two people were made homeless. The head of the family explained how he was returning from work at midday, the day before, when troops swarmed into the village. A jeep, with a loud speaker declared a curfew. The owner of the house said in arabic, which was then translated, that he was called to help people down the road clear their furniture out of their house. As he was about to do this he had to rush back finding his house full of troops. They were pulling the plugs out of the T.V. and refrigerator and driving the women and children out. Some of the troops were beating the young men, one of whom suffered had head wounds and was rushed to hospital. Half an hour was given to clear the furnishings. "Why? Why?" the owner asked. "How could this happen just out of the blue!" An officer came and demanded, "Where is your son Jehad?" Jehad, his son, was in prison and had been there without trial since early November. The soldier claimed that the owner's son was responsible for petrol bomb attacks on collaborators and soldiers. The house, built only ten years ago, was blown up.

Three large tents were erected close to the ruins. As we were going one young man, who spoke English, put this hand on my arm restraining me. He began weeping. He said he had two young children and a wife. They had saved for years to build the house. His two year old boy was saying over and over again, "The Jews have broken the whole earth!"

We left to see one other house where eighteen people had lost their homes and later saw one other smaller house destroyed. The destruction of the four houses had made sixty people homeless in one village. The price of the uprising is a dear one.

Further stress and suffering are associated specifically with the effects of civil disobedience. Cars either remain hidden or are impounded if taxes are not paid. New licenses and new license plates are now necessary. A new license is very costly and cannot be issued unless taxes are paid. Those Palestinians that arrange new license plates show clearly to their fellow countryman they have paid their taxes. Nor does the military administration just pressure individuals. A colleague of mine, who was awarded a full academic scholarship to go abroad, was not given permission because his brother had not paid his taxes. The restrictions on the amounts of money Palestinians can bring from Jordan continue and as incomes have fallen here, the controls make life more difficult. Schools and Universities continue to be closed although kindergartens are functioning. Frequently, I meet students who are becoming increasingly frustrated wanting to complete their degree as to start some job or career.

And it is not as if I just read or listened about these sufferings. I have seen them. I have seen and heard the cry of agony as a young man was hit by a bullet and died two days later. The soldiers only fired three shots in that incident. They were in no danger. I have seen the wounds in the Handicapped Center in Bethlehem and in a small way I tried to nurse broken limbs back to life. I witness their pain, their despair and depressions. Yet they can still smile, even the totally innocent. Of Hussain, in a car in no way involved in a demonstration the dum dum bullet went through the car door into his leg. Of Suleiman, only twelve years old, his right leg amputated. He was leaving school when the older boys were demonstrating in the street. Of Yousef, a very likable young man with three bullet fragments in his head. How many more have I seen? A girl struck in the top of her neck with a plastic bullet and now virtually paralyzed, a quadriplegic. Quite true, the very stones should cry out but the world press only sees ten to fifteen percent of what is happening. Nor do I make mention of the deaths, miscarriages and permanent illnesses caused by the teargases, particularly those used in enclosed places. I do not mention the women political prisoners, their beatings and torture. Nor have I really demonstrated the suffering and inhumanity of long curfews in villages or camps, or investigated the fifty-eight deportation orders issued since the Intifada began of which thirty-four have been deported and the remainder are still pending. I have touched on the suffering of families and individuals and hinted at the effect Israeli restrictions have had on education and economic activity.

I write with a certain frustrated anguish and anger at all the suffering. My daily reading of the Jerusalem Post, the Amnesty International Report of 17th August 1988, of the Human Rights Association report dated 7th October 1988, of friends who work in the Red Cross and the Al-Haq, Law in the Services of Man's report on "Dahriyyeh: Centre for Punishment," published in May 1988, all make harrowing reading and listening.

I think it was in Peter Shaffer's play where Equus explains quite simply "I need a way of seeing in the dark." I recall the owner of one of the destroyed houses in El- Khader, as he talked to us of his tragedy repeatedly saying, "Hamdulillah, Hamdulillah!" (God be blessed, God be blessed).

"I tell you I have not seen such great faith!" Jesus said.

XVIII / GOD'S ON OUR SIDE. CHRISTMAS TIME IN BETHLEHEM 1988.

Carol music pervades the bright morning air. Bands and singers are already performing in Manger Square. From my window in what must be one of the finest panoramas of any house, I can see the mountains of Moab across the Dead Sea in Jordan. They stand out in the haze like a distant blue wall along the skyline. Below, the rectangular limestone buildings of Bethlehem are stacked up on the hillsides. The sun is warm; it is a beautiful day.

And yet to look more closely at the flat rooftops, another reality is apparent. The town is saturated with troops. The soldiers are numerous both on the ground and on the tops of buildings. No one wants trouble here; body searches are the regulation for the day if you desire to join the festivities in the Square and special passes are required to drive into and from Bethlehem through the numerous roadblocks. The Patriarch will arrive in the procession sometime after midday. Mass concelebrated will be with the Apostolic Delegate in the fine University chapel and the students of Hotel Management will put on a splendid reception afterwards.

As I write two F-16's glitter in the sunlight as they roll through the blue sky down into the rift valley, now mere black silhouettes thundering over the distant Dead Sea. A strange land this, full of ambiguities and irony. Peace on earth and Goodwill to all men! A happy Christmas and New Year to everyone.

How trite! I wrote the above three years ago when Christmas, inspite of the heavy security was a celebration. A pall of sadness cast its gloom over Bethlehem this Christmastime 1988, the second year of the Intifada.

Even more troops than usual invaded the town. More road blocks, more body checks, more house searches, more arrests of people who might put the peace at risk and an overwhelming blanket of security stifled the life of the local population. Opposite the Tantur Institute and situated on the side of the road just before it enters the West Bank and Bethlehem, an increasingly large army encampment developed over the weeks into something of permanence. More tents, more trucks, more jeeps, generators, and cooking equipment appeared and people said under their breaths that a new settlement may well be established as the bulldozers flattened the terraces and the scattered olive trees, where the mayor of Bethlehem had planned to build football and other recreational facilities. These would have been the only public sporting facilities open to the young people of Bethlehem. Here cars were stopped and the military computer checked to see if the drivers had paid their taxes. As the days went by more and more cars and trucks were impounded not only because taxes were not paid but the new car licences were not purchased or the new Intifada taxes not collected to pay for the occupation.

Christian Palestinians did not celebrate Christmas. There were no decorations in the homes, no lights in the streets, no Christmas tree in the Square, no attractive presentations in the shops (though the Military Governor called all the shopkeepers together to put pressure on them to make their shops colourful, they did not comply) and the same was true of each family. There would be no Christmas cards, no presents, no visit of Father Christmas, nor parties or celebrations. The Israelis tried to cheer the few tourists that did venture to Bethlehem with more coloured lights than usual in Talpiot, a Jerusalem suburb, which borders the Green-Line that is the boundary with the West Bank.

For Christmas Eve the pamphlet from the Unified Leadership of the Intifada called a general strike which in fact became virtually a curfew. The rain poured down and a thick whirling mist smothered the town for the whole of the Latin Christmas period. The troops must have had a wretched time as the clouds unloaded their cargoes hour after hour. Sentry duty on the roof tops must have been a wretched business. Visibility at times was only a few yards, particularly when the strong winds abated. So it was that people began to say to each other that God was on the side of the Intifada.

The customary arrival of the Latin Patriarch was surrounded by a web of politics. The Military Governor was insisting on the arrangements that were part of the Status Quo. The Christians debated whether there should be any entrance by the Patriarch into Bethlehem at all. The press was manipulated by the Israelis attempting to give the impression that normality reigned when in fact the Patriarch came in a small column of cars with none of the usual bands and boy scouts and was only greeted by the officials in Manger Square and a small crowd of tourists. On Christmas Eve there was the traditional Midnight Mass in the church of St. Catherine but people I know who went there were disappointed in the almost unpleasant atmosphere created by the tight security and sense of unease with the formal presence of the Military Governor and other Israeli representatives.

For the expatriates of the University staff, we celebrated Midnight Mass at the Mar Andrea university property where the sisters' accommodation and girls students' hostel are situated. I was delegated to pick up one of the staff who is Scottish and her young Palestinian husbana and new born baby. Perhaps one of the more memorable moments for all of us was when husband, wife and infant entered the chapel a little late (we had trouble starting the car because of the cold wet weather) looking as though they were the Holy Family. The father, his head covered with a red and white kaffiyeh and his dark bearded Palestinian face looking down at the baby well covered with warm blankets walked to the front of the chapel. All eyes turned and there were smiles on the worshipers' faces.

At two thirty in the morning I drove them home in the company of a Franciscan priest. After leaving their house returning to the Hebron road from Beit Jala, we saw huddled groups of people drenched in the driving rain. A strong wind was blowing and the mist had lifted and had been driven away. They were French pilgrims desperate to get back to their hotels in Jerusalem. Well, Christmas spirit had its persuasive powers and with a certain risk involved, because I was driving an Arab registered car, we negotiated the check points at Tantur and deposited them at Jaffa Gate by the Old City. One of the group was a French journalist from the Le Monde paper. On our return in most treacherous conditions, with the wind howling and the rain worse than ever, we witnessed small groups of pilgrims struggling in the inclement weather quite deliberately walking to Bethlehem for the 4:30 a.m. Mass at the Nativity.

The virtual closure of Bethlehem was repeated about a week later when the Greek Orthodox celebrated their Christmas. Then the Armenian Christians have their feast which really is the Epiphany commemorating the visit of the Magi. Again stringent measures are taken by the occupying force to prevent any disruptions. I am sure the Israelis soldiers would recommend, though for different motives than I, the abolition of three Christmases and the amalgamation into one feast.

It was during the Christmas time that we, as a community, decided we should do more to help the people around us. A large portion of our nominal salaries went back into the University. We did, however have some surplus monies so at one of our community meetings we decided to form a committee to dispose of the surplus as urgent needs came to our attention.

The handicapped centre, run on voluntary funding was in desperate need of a steriliser; our Brothers' community supplied this. Student contacts put us in touch with families who had no heating in the very cold weather. Oil heaters were purchased and several dozen families were given a more tolerable environment to live in, especially in the refugee camps.

We were told about our student Yousif, mentioned earlier in the narrative, whose house was blown up. The young man, full of initiative had started to rebuild his house. The military stepped in refusing to allow him to build on the site where his house had been, even though his family had owned the land for generations. Immediately a military order for confiscation of the land was made. Undeterred Yousif purchased another plot of land but then ran out of money for the building materials. We agreed to purchase 1000 dollars worth of steel for the construction. Work commenced and on fine days he and some friends would be found on the building on the site.

Also sleeping bags were purchased for one of the villages near Bethlehem where several houses had been demolished. Again, in a few cases help was given with food and where new heaters were supplied, a quantity of oil, enough to last out the winter. Most of the purchasing was undertaken by some of our mature students who were also responsible for the distribution of the goods. Our contribution was but a drop in the ocean and we really wished to do more, such was the hardship and suffering around us.

The Christmas message of Michel Sabbah, the Latin Patriarch of Jerusalem was, nevertheless, one of hope. He said that "on this feast of peace and joy, to the people of the Holy Land, we say, secure borders can only be secure if hearts are reconciled. Secure borders are not secured by technology, or by violence, or occupied territories. Only reconciled hearts, love and truth make secure borders." His message was one trusting in the goodness of man, even though he recognised how Christian Palestinians had no joy at Christmas because many had suffered the loss of a son or father killed; others were still in prisons, and all faced a heavy military repression. He addressed himself to both peoples, Israelis and Arab, saying that legitimate aspirations must be recognised and that both peoples must free themselves from fear and begin to trust each other. These sentiments required a great fund of faith and hope on the part of the inhabitants on both sides of the Green-Line.

XIX / THE DAY BETHLEHEM WENT UPSIDE DOWN

"Bethlehem is turned upside down!" cried some young Arab boys to Father Peter, a Jesuit priest who teaches at the University, as he returned to Bethlehem this Saturday morning. Bethlehem certainly had inverted itself. I don't recall anything quite like it during the whole disturbed year of the Intifada.

Saturday morning proved to be an eventful one. I had an appointment with Mayor Freij in the municipal offices. He had heard about my articles in The Tablet, a Catholic magazine in the United Kingdom, and wanted to see copies of them. A colleague of mine had seen the mayor of Bethlehem the previous day when he was making representations to him, on behalf of a father of a Palestinian family whose house was to be destroyed the following Tuesday by order of the Military Governor. Apparently he was walking through the village of Ortas when the father of a family of ten children called to him desperately seeking help. The house was built on land bought in 1973. The military authorities now suddenly declared there was no record for the purchase of the land nor was there permission for the house. During the Intifada several hundred houses had been destroyed under this pretence, in addition to the 150 destroyed for reasons of collective punishment. In arranging an interview for this villager and in discussing the general situation, my name came the mayor's attention.

The Palestinian gate keeper at the entrance of the University told me not to leave the property. I was hoping to walk down to the Manger Square for my 8:45 appointment and was reluctant to miss it. "Mish kwayyes!" he urged,"Mish kwayyes!" I ventured out into Frères Street to find a series of stone barricades across the road, burning tyres by the convent school and masked youths with stones. Kindergarten children with their parents were scurrying home from St. Joseph's convent. Nearby scores of boys and girls from the secondary schools on the Hebron Road had been dismissed because of the death of a 15 year old boy. The army bombarded the children with tear gas. At the bottom of Children's Street over twenty troops were pouring into Azza refugee camp. Later I was to find out they were searching for the body of a 15 year old boy Nabil Abu-Laban, who had been shot in the Deheisha refugee camp and whose family had spirited it away very early that morning from the Jabel

Da'ud Hospital. The whole of Bethlehem appeared to be in a state of turmoil. Discretion being the better part of valour I retreated behind the high walls of the University,which incidentally are covered in English graffiti, the recent work of Israeli soldiers.

Later in the morning I took a chance and with a companion walked down to The Manger Square. The stone barriers were still occupied with young men and in some cases girls of no more than 15 years of age. A young man who spoke fluent English warned us not to take photographs. We explained we were from the University and said we knew the family of the boy that had died and that we did not have a camera. The Manger Square was full of troops, jeeps and a sinister half-track that carried a stone firing machine on its upper structure. Close by was a tourist bus with pilgrims who were peacefully pacing their way towards the Church of The Nativity seemingly oblivious to the real world around them.

Shortly before we entered the Municipal building, Mayor Freij arrived with several ambulances. We were ushered into his reception room. Seconds later, he bustled into the room, a short authoritative figure. He was under great pressure, he said. The America Consul was just arriving. Apparently the army was impeding the ambulances from collecting the injured and taking them to the hospitals. Mayor Freij had then appealed to the American Consulate. He was most anxious that I talk to the doctor responsible. Doctor Hikmat Abu Rdeineh explained that the five Bethlehem ambulances were stopped by the soldiers forcing the drivers out and, in some instances, taking the ingnition keys of the vehicles. This tactic had been going on for several weeks and seriously injured people were delayed, in some cases, for more than half an hour. Army interference meant that most casualties were taken to the hospitals in private transport. Inspite of this, the doctor said, the records showed 108 journeys were made in 1988 carrying victims with gunshot wounds: 80 unconscious casualties from tear gases and 70 individuals with fractures and broken bones during the last calender year; all these injuries were the result of the Intifada in the Bethlehem area. The doctor said that in his view, the real Intifada had just started.

Saturday evening, after Mass and dinner we gathered round the fire listening to the various experiences of the day. One of our guests, a French nurse from the Caritas baby hospital described how their social workers were desperately trying to help the Bedouin families that lived in a village near the aggressive settlement of Kiriat Arba. Late in October 1988, 27 of the 32 houses in their village were destroyed by the Israelis. On Christmas Day the appalling weather blew away the light tents housing 500 people exposing them to the freezing rain and wind. The nurse also said that one of the Italian sisters from the hospital bought a large supply of sleeping bags for the homeless Bedouin from West

Jerusalem. When she was asked by the Israeli supplier who they were for, she explained there were a large number of orphans requiring warm bedding. The French nurse also mentioned that the social workers at the Caritas hospital usually dealt with 200 needy families a year. In the last six months 900 families had received, help and the stock of clothing provided by pilgrim groups had been severely depleted.

Other stories of the day included the entry into the St. Joseph's convent by the soldiers when one of the sisters was saying goodbye to graduate friends. The students were from Gaza. Only the heated shouting at the troops saved the completely innocent young people from a beating and arrest. Contact was also made with a student in a village beyond the Herodion. Two of the Brothers on the staff had an important message to pass on to her. They did not have the correct address and drove out into the desert towards a Bedouin village called Ubeidiya only to find themselves impeded by a stone barrier across the road in a remote valley. On looking up the slope of the valley they discovered ten, twenty, thirty young men with frightening masks over their heads and slings at the ready. Only a breezy greeting in Arabic and the inquiry as to the correct village where the girl lived, saved the searchers from further embarrassment. The leader of the group gave them insructions to drive to Zatara a village that extends well into the desert. Eventually her home was found on the white-brown limestone hills that are high enough to give a view of the rift valley. Rula was famous in her village. She was the first young person to go to the University and the village had a day of celebration in her honour.

It was another woman member of the University staff who lectures very effectively training student social workers, who shared her most recent observations on the social structure of the Palestinian family. She said that the Intifada not only caused a certain chaos to everyday life but it was rapidly changing the roles within the Palestinian family. The traditional family hierachy was being turn upside down. Relationships between parents and children, husband and wife, the once revered elders and the young people, and between girls and boys, was undergoing a profound change. It seem that the young boys were fast becoming the leaders in many families with father often out of work (recent research apparently shows that 70% of those Arab men working in Israel have lost their jobs) and losing face with frequent humiliations and stresses laid upon them. Further internal stresses gave the women increasingly stronger roles. Frequently, it is the mother who protests and argues with the soldiers or the daughter who runs errands instead of the boy for whom it would not be safe.

The external pressures made by school closures cause the young to miss the controlled situation and socialisation associated with forming human values in the school environment. Exposure to the very high rate of violence is reflected in the games the children play and in their dreams. Where the TV news showed how four Palestinians were buried alive by the soldiers in the famous Kfar Salim incident, a family of young Palestinian children buried alive their new born sister because of the jealousy her arrival instigated. Idealization of the stone thrower, the fame of the wounded, and the ambition on the part of some of the young to become martyrs, further cause the loss of prestige of the parents and elders who had held the status quo for over twenty years. Parents are torn between the ideals of nationhood and the struggle for survival. In many cases the village elders are discredited, their passiveness considered apathetic by the superactive young.

The degree of change of roles and hierarchy within the Palestinian family depended to some extent on where the family was situated, whether in a village, a camp, or a large town. Also the extent of the change was related to the frequency and intensity of the confrontation with the occupying power and its army.

Though the Intifada had certainly improved the cohesion, collective concern, identity, self esteem and character of the Palestinians, observers and researchers of the social scene were worried that the tensions might produce a pathological society. Though a vast number of young people were gaining in leadership and responsibility, they were still getting double messages from their parents. Whom am I supposed to love? Am I supposed to hate? If I'm supposed to help, to help whom?

So this was the Saturday when Bethlehem went "upside down." It was also the day when the media informed us that the tectonic plates in the Jordan Rift valley were due to adjust themselves and a minor earth tremor of five was expected on the Richter scale. We had also read the Sunday Gospel where the water was changed into wine. I rarely remember much in the homily at Mass these days but I'm sure we prayed in the bidding prayers for change, a change of heart, and I rather recall someone praying for another miracle.

XX / DISTANCE TEACHING AND TAKING RISKS

To say we met in an upper room in the Old City of Jerusalem would bring other stories to mind of final suppers or fearful Apostles waiting for the Holy Spirit to inspire them. There were seven of us. We had not seen each other for 15 months. What a joy to meet my students again. We were attempting to complete their degree courses now delayed by more than a year and a quarter. They were either third or fourth year undergraduates anxious to get down to serious work and to have some chance of finding a job or starting a career. We had entered the empty house belonging to the family of one of the students. Surreptitiously we had climbed the stairs from one of the narrow lanes that are typical of the Old City. Just up the street was the Latin Patriarchate where waiting students had sheltered out of sight so as not to attract the attention of the soldiers.

This was my Jerusalem class. The room was well furnished and we sat down on comfortable arm chairs, and the student responsible for the house had provided a fire and some drinks and cakes. This meeting or class would be considered illegal by the military authorities and we were all subject to arrest. So there had been considerable concern on the part of the University administration both for the students and for the staff who were involved in the six week distance learning and teaching course. It was made quite clear to us that although the University had initiated the programme, they could do nothing to protect us. Both the staff and students embarked on the adventure voluntarily and were not under any strict obligation. Although there were many misgivings and fears, particularly and understandably so from some of the Palestinian staff, the great majority asked rallied round and participated. It was only natural that there was an air of fear and conspiracy as we opened our literature books and embarked on a course so violently interrupted at the end of October 1987 when Isaac was shot dead on the University campus.

Earlier I had met the Bethlehem class of six students in a hotel. It was a strange experience being ushered up on the lift by a nervous manager and directed into an empty hotel bar on the fourth floor to teach Victorian Literature to a predominately Moslem group of students. Half way through the class there was shooting outside that did not help concentrate the mind on Tennyson's "In

Memoriam" and later "The Lady of Shalott," when a riot took place in the street below. For the next meeting we changed location and obtained permission to hold classes in a hospital. The occasional crying infant was more acceptable. Nevertheless, a worried matron drew down the blinds so no one could see in, and we had to switch on the lights.

Some preparation had been made before for the staff who taught third or fourth year students, to commence teaching. Members of the administration had flown to England to the Open University for advice. It became obvious that we could use very little of the sophistication or have the wealth of experience currently operating from Milton Keynes. It would require years of preparation for a fully developed distance learning operation. It was unlikely that this could be set up easily in a society with so many of the characteristics of a developing third world country. Further still, the level of sophistication in communications required could hardly be attained when the people were involved in an uprising. Such things as basic telephone links either did not exist or were cut. The University telephones had been out of operation for over a year. Under military occupation radio and television were out of the question too. Nevertheless, our education department gave courses to all those who were involved in the new teaching programme, in an attempt to facilitate the planning and running of courses under the new conditions.

In practice the experience reminded me more of sixth form teaching or of university tutorials in the British system. The teacher worked closely with a small intimate group. Student participation was high and the amount of work and the level of understanding encouraging. This was a far better learning situation than lecturing to a class of thirty.

The distance learning element should have come into operation when students were unable to attend classes. Taha, one of the students from the far north of the country and from a village called Kalkilia, where four young men had been killed (including one of our students) was under curfew on two occasions when lessons were given. He would have found it very difficult to study on his own, such are the demands of Victorian texts for foreign students. I will be interested to see whether any part of the distance learning operated successfully in his situation.

A start was made at the beginning of January. Teachers were allocated classes of five to six students which would meet for a minimum of six times in six weeks and attempt to complete a 2 or 3 unit course. Off-campus locations were hard to find, and when the schools were closed again indefinitely by the military(the media of course said it was the civilian government which in fact is run by the military) there was an acute shortage of locations. Contacting the students was left to the individual teacher. Fortunately, the Arab society has a remarkable ability to communicate by word of mouth. Students who had heard indirectly gathered at the gate of the University anxious to know who their teacher was and where and what they were to be taught. They could only be taught subjects that they had registered for 15 months ago and for which they had books. It was obvious too, that many of the courses involving laboratories and practical work had to wait.

Nothing is ever secret in the Palestinian society. As more and more students virtually appeared on the streets near the University, individuals were obviously nervous that the Israelis would take this as an affront to their authority and stamp out the work. Everyone just hoped that the work could continue as it became obvious that with the closure of the schools there would be no chance of the University opening.

To renew friendships with the Palestinian student was always a pleasure. In my Bethlehem class was Yousif, the remarkable young man who had his house destroyed. He was cheerful and became the leader of the group. A leader was necessary to arrange contacts, to supervise additional photocopying, and generally to be the communicator between the students and the teacher and between the students themselves.

Then there was Rula from the village near the Herodion called Za'atra, whom I searched for a week previously. She was very shy and diffident having to work with fourth year men since she was only in the third year, a Junior, as the American college system described them. She found the work very difficult and it took time to get her to participate actively in the lessons. It was during one of the later lessons well into the six weeks that she was noticeably depressed. At the mid-afternoon break I asked her if anything was wrong. She quietly told me that seven houses in her village of Za'atra and six houses in a neighbouring villages of Obeidiyah and Fureidis had been destroyed by bulldozers. When I asked the reasons for the demolitions she explained they did not have licences. This was a distressingly all too familiar tale. The latest figures for housing demolition numbered, according to one source, nearly 360 buildings during the period of the Intifada. This news really took the enthusiasm out of my teaching that afternoon.

Another attractive young woman from a Bethlehem family was Nadia. She also was in the third year and found Browning's dramatic monologues very difficult. I had a suspicion she had something on her mind which she finally declared to the group three weeks later. She had to own up to the fact that she had not done the written work for that week which was an essential part of the distance learning programme. The following evening she was to be engaged, she said, and the preparation and excitement had occupied her mind. It lead me to reflect that the number of engagements and marriages appeared to be increasing as the Intifada progressed. I was to discover later that two of the women students in the Jerusalem group were also engaged.

As the course progressed I discovered how it was essential to find out what was happening in the lives of the students. Two of the men in the Bethlehem group were teachers in Hebron. Just before the schools were ordered shut again in the middle of January 1989, in the new year, they both had unpleasant experiences. Both of them had demonstrations in their respective schools. In one, a settler shot three students when they got outside the school and threw stones at his bus. Troops arrived closing the school and taking all the staff to the military headquarters. Here interrogations took place and when teachers refused to give names of their students, they were forced to perform humiliating actions, such as standing on one leg until they fell over; then finally the military, having failed to obtain any information, abruptly dismissed them.

The second teacher, a married man with two children, had a similar experience in his school. He also had to cope with the death of his nephew who was shot in a demonstration. His concentration during the afternoon lesson was not enhanced by the unpleasant experiences driving to Bethlehem. At a check point on the Hebron road he was ordered out of his car, was kicked and had his identity card taken from him.

From the short experience of teaching students off campus, it became quite obvious to me that if the university opened it would hardly be able to function for long, such was the unrest and the constant provocation to which the students were subjected. It was going to require a great deal of concentration to study and follow the academic work related to the small studious, orderly groups in off-campus situations. Normal university life seemed unrealistic until a political solution could be made that would defuse the situation. Some staff argued that we should not risk teaching off campus, not through fear of arrest but because, they reasoned, the Israelis would use our activities as propaganda, telling the world that they were allowing the universities to function.

As the course progressed I became aware of the further difficulties particularly with the male students. Akram came all the way from a village outside Jenin which was in the northernmost part of the West Bank. He travelled at great expense and was subject to body searches as he left his village, as the bus left Ramallah and then he suffered a further indignity at the gates of the Old City. It was obvious he could not bring any notes or books with him. I rearranged the lessons having two two-hour lessons on Friday in Jerusalem so that he could stay with friends the night and return on Saturday to his village making one awkward journey rather than two in one week.

It was only yesterday when I was walking through New Gate in the Old City of Jerusalem to teach my class, that I witnessed first hand the appalling treatment the young male Palestinians suffer. Green beret Border Police, a tough element in the Israeli security forces, were stationed by the gate interrogating young Palestinian men, taking their identity cards and lining them up against the wall. They were then threatening the men and taking them one by one into the small toilet in the wall just to the left of the gate. Here, and I stood and witnessed it, they beat the Arabs with their fists and batons. I had known this was going on for some time but had never actually witnessed it. The shop keepers had complained to me many times, and on several occasions one of them was so sickened by the brutality and intimidation, he had closed his shop and returned home. Another shop keeper had telephoned the police on a number of occasions to no avail. I was so incensed that I challenged one of the soldiers and asked him what the young men had done to deserve such treatment. I was brushed aside and told to mind my own business.

I had to pass the Latin Patriarchate on the way to the house where I was teaching so I went in to complain to the secretary and asked him to forward my protest to the Patriarch when he returned from Rome. I argued that this was the Christian quarter of the Old City and surely we should not just allow this to happen without some protest. When I met my students I muttered to them when they asked me how I was: "Ana zalan, ana zalan!" (I'm angry, angry.)

I then learnt a salutary lesson. With a gentle smile and with the graciousness that I found so appealing, a student from Nablus explained. "Brother Patrick this really is nothing. Come to Nablus; this happens everyday." Another student then asked him to explain what he discovered when he went home after last week's lesson and his overnight stay in Bethlehem. "When I arrived home on the Saturday morning I found my mother in a very disturbed condition. Whilst I was attending your lesson the soldiers came to my house, arrested both my brothers and my cousin, smashed the furnishings and glasses and plates and poured our precious supplies of flour, sugar and salt into one mixed mess on floor." I was just astonished at his calm manner. "How can you say that and smile?" I said. He looked at me patiently and explained, "What else can I do ?"

Some of the University staff who complained about having to get to their lessons at eight in the morning were quite overwhelmed when students of theirs left the Gaza Strip at 4:00 a.m. in the morning in order to attend the lesson of two hours and then return to their camps on another three-hour journey. Another example of student determination was to travel during the strikes to lessons when there was no transportation available. One student walked through the hills from his village of Beit Ummar to Bethlehem to complete a lesson and then returned on foot. When young people make this sort of effort and play down their sacrifices in a very modest manner, present themselves in a gentle and cheerful way, one is quite overwhelmed by their courage and simplicity and feels spurred on to do one's best for them.

I sometimes wondered about the relevance of the Victorian Literature course that I taught. It made me reflect too on some of the implications of the blanket closures on all the schools and places of further education. At the time of writing 300,000 school age children are without classes, as well as 18,000 university and community college students. Students of all ages make up approximately 40% of the total population of the West Bank and probably an even higher proportion on the Gaza Strip. The closures force one to think of some of the more basic socialising disciplines students acquire at school irrespective of the importance of syllabuses. I am sure that although the students I taught found Victorian writing hard, there were some gains to be made from studying the literature, not only in touching on some of the major 19th century ideas that effected the 20th century, but in the gathering of minds for a specific academic and socialising activity. Obviously content of syllabus should be relevant to the students needs but the mere fact of coming together for an educational purpose spoke volumes for me and, I think, for the students in the hectic and sometimes very difficult environment in which we found ourselves.

In the sequence of events that affected education and led up to the first long closure of the schools during the uprising, the Israeli Minister of Defence, Mr. Rabin warned: "We will close schools which have ceased to fulfill their function as educational institutions and which have been consistent with having allowed their children on the streets." It was true that as the situation became worse many schools did become centres of unrest.

But this was patently untrue for many places that were fulfilling their role. It was certainly true, too, of many schools before the second severe closure in January in 1989. Parents, teachers, and children were dismayed by the blanket closures. Where there was unrest it was often provoked by the presence of soldiers very close to the schools. Only today as I write this, school heads and leaders in the Gaza Strip were making representations to the Military Governor there making the plea that if the troops were taken away there would be less likelihood of a disturbance. This was certainly true of my experiences at the University before the Intifada. When students, on one occasion were deliberately starting a protest, the soldiers did not turn up, and they were then at loss as to know what to do and the whole situation was defused.

Just before Christmas the Al-Haq, Law in the Service of Man association, published a report called " Punishing a Nation." In this detailed report it examined the legality of Israeli measures to suppress the education of the young Palestinian people. The lawyers argued a strong case, not only quoting international law, the Geneva Convention, the Hague Regulations (specifically Article 56) but also the local Jordanian Law that governed education on the

West Bank, demonstrating that prolonged closures were illegal and that to suppress the alternative forms of education was against the basic principles of human rights.

However, when the widespread closures took place on the 3rd February 1988 some schools and universities started alternative forms of education. Small groups met, just like we were attempting in Bethlehem and in Jerusalem, and were declared illegal and were promptly raided. The arrests made of staff and students at Al-Najah University in Nablus was an example.

In addition to the closures of the schools The Al-Haq Law in the Service of Man was quite clear in its claim that the use of schools as temporary military posts, or the raids made on schools were illegal and violated Article 56 of the Hague Regulations. With these observations about the application of law to a nation under occupation and my own belief in the rule of law, I felt free in my conscience to be of service to the young students for whom I was responsible.

And it is obvious with the frequent interrogation of staff and students the the Israeli authorities know exactly what we are doing. I think it is a case that we know that they know that we know and so on. In the final analysis the Israeli action is about control. The occupying force must been seen to be in charge. How long we will be allowed to continue the off campus teaching remains to be seen. Maybe if we are discreet we may manage to survive and complete some of the undergraduates' courses. Who knows? This is a land of unpredictability.

After the lesson yesterday in the Old City, I walked with one of the students up the narrow lane past the courtyard at the entrance to the Latin Patriarchate, round the corners near the Pontifical Mission Headquarters, then to the the familiar shop fronts of Sinora's, the butchers, now closed for the Friday afternoon strike, down the street where the College de Frères stands and smartly out of New Gate past the soldiers who were waiting for their truck to return them to their barracks.

He happened to be the student from Nablus. We caught the same service (a taxi which runs rather like a bus service and is extremely cheap transport) to Bethlehem. We listened to the amusing conversation between the driver and his passengers about the service fares. The driver was complaining that the price of oil and gas had gone up but the fares were the same. The passengers, of course were not too sympathetic, and so the discussion got quite excited but the good humour remained. I wondered too what was going through my student friend's mind when the discussion turned to the steep rise in prices of basic foodstuffs like floor, sugar and salt. We reached Bethlehem. He said good-bye saying he would see me next week. He said with a smile, he would have the essay that was due this Friday ready for me next week. "Inshallah" (God willing), I said.

XXI / THE ARENA

Our house has a wonderful view across the southern slopes of Bethlehem. I have described in enthusiastic terms the panorama that extends into Jordan including the undulating desert ridges, the depression marking the Rift valley and the blue mountains of Moab, observed clearly, especially after the occurence of rains which remove the dust in the atmosphere and so enhance the visibility for the onlooker. What I have not mentioned or described is the immediate middle ground just below us. This I call the arena.

Why? You may ask. Well, first it has the shape of an arena. The limestone ridge has a large embayment cut into it resulting in a extensive amphitheatre with its base facing the busy Manger Road. Manger Road, certainly only built after 1950, makes one of its many sweeping curves at this point, in its passage for traffic bound for Manger Square and the centre of the town. Rising up on a gradual gradient is the old main road that for centuries climbed the northern end of the long ridge on which much of Bethlehem is built. This is Star Street:famous Star Street. This road would have taken Crusaders and pilgrims over the centuries for about a quarter of a mile from this spot to the main gates and wall of Bethlehem. The narrow winding street is tightly constrained by the walls of houses and should really be a one way road. The tunnel-like gate in the wall remains just beside the bakery.

Not only does the morphology of the location lend itself to the description "arena", but so also does its chequered history. The place is known by the local Palestinians as Ras Fteiss. Translated from the Arabic, this means, the place of The Stinking Head. "How odd," I said to myself when this first came to my notice, surely this is another one of those local myths. Further investigation demonstrated a derivation based on the historical tradition that several battles were fought here and presumably Crusader and Moslem bodies lay dismembered after the fighting close to the main gates of the town.

Just as I write this, I am not exaggerating, a series of shots ring out in the area I have described. It is 3:45 p.m., February 1st, 1989. The middle ground below our high vantage point is the latest battlefield. If you want to witness the daily version of the uprising as it drags on well into its second year, take a seat on our balcony, and observe a mini Intifada unfold before you.

For months now, often several times a day, groups of masked youths, sometimes teenagers, occasionally young boys no older than ten, set up their constant challenge to the army. Because the amphitheatre overlooks the busy Manger Road, stone throwers take advantage of its position to bombard military vehicles and settlers' cars. Besides Star Street, there are two other small streets and several alleyways near the vantage point.

All is carefully orchestrated. The large garbage containers, which have wheels (dozens of these containers, a gift from the German Government to the municipality of Bethlehem, are located at strategic places all over the town) are dragged and overturned by the youths. Then stones are built up across the roads rendering them impassable. Incidentally, friends, who have never been to the Holy Land wonder at the inexhaustible supply of stones used by the Palestinians during the uprising. A visit here, and they will soon realise, that the geology of the land is made up of marine limestones. Dry stone walls are everywhere and the stockpile seemingly endless. The nearest illustration for a British traveller would to remind him or her of the patterns of dry stone walls in the Pennines.

All the roads are blocked. Lookouts are posted up to over half a mile away. The troops radio that stoning has started on Manger Road. A series of whistles pierce the air and the signals are given that troops are on the way. Jeeps rush to the area only to find their passage blocked. More army trucks and in some cases jeeps are now equipped with bulldozing fixtures to bash through the barriers. Nevertheless the soldiers, whatever their tactics, are generally too late. I have seen what looked like nine year olds scamper away like monkeys down the slopes of the "Arena" with fit young soldiers giving chase; I have yet to see one caught. The houses in the neighbourhood suffer from the constant and sometimes serious problems caused by clouds of tear gas and are liberally sprayed with what appear to be rubber bullets and sometimes live plastic ammunition.

If the youth of Bethlehem have developed some level of sophistication the wider perspective or arena on the West Bank shows organisation on a larger scale. For example, in the Casbah of Nablus, where well organised teams are established, there are in each area three distinct teams. First, there are the offensive teams that throw the stones. These are fit young men, who incidently are divided into left hand throwers and right hand throwers. The arches of the Casbah are so situated that to take cover and throw stones requires a left handed person in specific positions and a right in others. Then there are defensive teams who cover the retreating offensive groups. Finally, a third team, largely composed of women, are strategically placed to send messages, whistle warnings and to rush soldiers that are attempting to arrest young men or boys who are caught.

These teams composed of women are significant for several reasons. First they harass the Israeli soldiers. How do you react, if you are a soldier, to a group of women frantically claiming their sons and dragging their offspring away? There is the true story in Ramallah of an American mother, married to a Palestinian, jumping on the jeep where her son was about to be arrested and driven off. Wildly displaying her American passport she confounded the officer on the jeep. What became a bit too much for the young soldier was when another woman, a genuine Palestinian, dressed in the traditional dress, also flung herself onto the moving vehicle claiming the arrested boy was her son too! A second result of this type of intervention by the women has been the Israeli response. Apparently, the troops are now issued with sprays that are directed at the faces of the women and which are used to stun them and incapacitate them. It is not difficult to visualize that the role of women during the Intifada has changed significantly and that their status, once very inferior in the family hierarchy and in society at large, has transformed beyond all recognition.

It is misleading to think that the Intifada is just a form of protest expressed in stone throwing. Perhaps it has become a symbol, whether it occurs on a micro scale in the small arena outside our windows each day or whether it is seen in a wider persepective over the whole of the West Bank and Gaza Strip. It is, after all, a small part of the whole reaction of the people, and basically the only widespread manifestation of violence. The presence of the Israeli army is mainly to enforce the wide ranging powers of the occupation at every level of life. The extent of non-violent activities of the uprising by the Palestinians are forgotten in the tragedies of the violent confrontations. The strikes, the refusal to pay taxes, the resignations from posts in the service of the various departments like the police, administrative posts such as the customs and excise officers, the refusal to purchase Israeli goods, far outweigh the more vigorous forms of protest.

The wider geographical picture of the West Bank reveals another manifestation of the real situation. There are over 400 villages scattered from the north around Jenin southwards around Nablus and Ramallah, in particular, and further south to Hebron. The Israeli army can only control on a day to day basis, about a hundred of these small clusters of population. These villages virtually declare their independence setting up road blocks, openly displaying flags and clearly out of the control of the army. They are known as "liberated" villages. We have visited these villages. Kufr-Rai, where one of our students was shot dead, is a memorable example. The occupying army periodically will make early morning or night raids on these centres. Sometimes paratroopers and other crack troops are used. The young men flee to the hills and are rarely captured. Eventually the soldiers leave and independence or liberation is again reclaimed. A Palestinian lawyer told me he saw a video in which four or five villages gathered to celebrate. There was a march pass of contingents of young men from each village and open rejoicing. The extent and scope of the peoples'movement is really quite beyond the Israeli army's control.

Will the Palestinian people be able to hold out? Although I hear businessmen in Bethlehem bemoan their losses and in some cases virtual ruin,economically the bulk of the people will survive. Though there are cases of hardship, most do have food and most do have shelter. Their conditions are better, much better, than many third world countries. Where there is a chance of breakdown, this possibility would be in a psychological collapse. So far this has not happened. When things appeared bad, events seemed to give people more encouragement. King Hussein's withdrawal from the Westbank proved to be, after initial alarm on the part of some, a very positive event. The diplomatic success of the PLO two months later gave a further surge of determination, especially the PNC in Tunis and the reassembled United Nations in Geneva finally resulting in the weakening of American resolve not to talk with the PLO leadership.

Perhaps, another development will be needed soon to sustain the movement. Now some progress must be made on the ground to give the people a further sense of purpose and achievement. Much has been achieved so far. The Palestinians are no longer afraid.

They have remarkable willingness to use new ideas and to experiment. Where before, changes may have evolved slowly, now the risk of failure is accepted and if one idea does not work, another is tried. There is unity, restraint, discipline and method which were quite inconceivable a year and a half ago. It is remarkable in this situation, when a settler's gun is captured by Palestinians, it is destroyed and not retained. It was General Dayyan who claimed in 1967, that the Israelis would leave the West Bank when the Arabs lined up at the bus stops. A shrewd remark made with a deep sociological understanding. I think a claim may be made that a sense of discpline has been achieved.

Unfortunately, the Israelis are far from being psychologically ready. They are caught in the trauma of fear and are retreating into positions that do not give much immediate hope. It was a perceptive Palestinian, who is in close contact with many Israelis, who really thought they needed their own intifada. Only a rethinking and liberating spirit and imaginative leadership would enable them to trust the Palestinians and recognise the real arena was a political and diplomatic one in which both peoples can find peace, justice and security.

Let me return to the idea of a stage or arena. "Unless you become like little children" may not always appear to be the best phrase to use in the context of what is happening here. For in the street the other day a three year old, carried in its father's arms, shouted in Arabic at an Israeli soldier closeby, " Long live Palestine!" The soldier turned around angrily. The father offered the three year old child to the soldier suggesting it should be taken and arrested and sent to prison. How easily the adult in us can be confounded! Perhaps it is the small things that children do that turn hearts. In a refugee camp near Ramallah, a group of young children started throwing stones. Soldiers arrived but the young people had vanished all accept for a diminuative seven year old who stood in the middle of the road with a Palestinian flag in his hand. Maybe it is the basic humanness in all of us that caused the next simple act to take place. The leader of the patrol, an Israeli captain, picked up the little fellow and kissed him.

XXII / CONVERSATIONS

It's 6:30 a.m. in our kitchen and Ash Wednesday,the 8th of February. Some of the community are out at Mass. Jokingly we call them "The early morning Christians." Some go to the Salesians at 6.00 a.m.., others to the Sisters of St Joseph at 7.00 a.m. There will be Mass and ashes in the house this evening too, for all of us.

It's an Intifada strike day, today and tomorrow. All is very quiet. The sun is up from the East in Jordan. It is cold outside and a fresh breeze is blowing. We have a good view from the window and balcony.

"They put the flags up again!" My breakfast companion refers to a very tall cypress tree behind a house the far side of the embankment between our hillside and the opposite slopes. "How do they get there? It's a most dangerous climb. And the two poles with the large flags, how on earth do they fix them to the top branches?" I observed.

The top of the cypress tree was pointed and very flimsy and yet two flags on poles fluttered prominently in the wind. The horizontal black, white and green bands juxtaposed to the red trianglar area adjoining the flag pole formed a colourful glitter in the early morning sun.

"The monkeys, they really are. Fancy shining there at night with two large poles and avoiding the troops." The area is well patrolled at night with jeeps circulating through the narrow roads training their search lights on the walls and windows of the sleeping residents. "I bet the army gets here quickly,"I said, "Those flags will be seen from quite a distance." Surely enough, before we had completed our meagre breakfast (an appropriate word for the day) jeeps arrived and soldiers started questioning the people knocking on doors and gathering them outside.

The flag was a symbol of nationhood. For the Palestinians the scene was heartening; for the Israelis it was another daily irritation in the unrelenting policing of the uprising. My breakfast companion finished his cereals and mused: "Like last time really. The troops will have to get one of those gadgets, you know those long poles with tweezer things on the end. Then they will have to get on the roof of the neighbouring house. I imagine that will take a while to organize."

I glanced up at the kitchen clock. "Time for prayers," I said. We washed our dishes and went to recite the morning office.

◆   ◆

"You dogs, you dogs, you utter dogs!" she screamed in a fury. Anger, shear blind anger overrode any fears she may have had. Yet she was the young unobtrusive woman in the flower shop down town; pleasant, courteous, help-ful, delicately arranging the carnations with pleasing care.

"You dogs," came the heated Arabic. "Yet even the stray dogs on the street respect our homes. They don't come off the streets and break in."

Her family had been out that Sunday morning. In their absence the troops were searching for the boys who had just vanished after the latest altercation. They were searching the homes. Finding the little house locked, they forced in the front door. The soldiers were still around when the family returned. Their unobtrusive and rather poor home was all they had. They felt invaded, what little they had exposed, their privacy invaded.

"Would you see your house smashed? Your home broken in?" she screamed. "You don't need one stone thrown at your thick heads. You need a hundred stones. When will you understand?"

Blank puzzled and helpless faces stared out under the helmets and plastic visors. Thin and small she confronted them in their winter combat overalls and heavy boots. They found an Egyptian Israeli, who could speak Arabic. He was sent to the lady to explain. He hardly managed to respond and attempt a conversation. Certainly a message had been communicated. A Palestinian would never have attacked soldiers verbally in such an unrestrained fashion before the Intifada.

◆   ◆

"I wish to see Brother Joe and Brother James." he said.

"They're out,"I replied. I had been called to the University gates. No student is allowed in under military order. Arrest, a common enough occurrence these days, would result if the students attempt to come near the environs of our house.

"I wish to speak with them; I was meant to see them several weeks ago," he explained. He, I recall, in the days when I taught him, nearly a year and a half ago before the closure, was a most conscientious young man. Always anxious to complete his work, punctual and concerned almost to the point of becoming an obsession. He would not miss an appointment.

"Why didn't you see them?" I inquired. He looked at me intently. He was weather beaten, his hands rough, he must have been working out in the fields, certainly exposed to the cold wind and the winter sun.

"It's a long story," he stated.

"Tell me," I answered. I knew he came from up in the hills in a village near Hebron. He had been lame from birth and walked with a distinct limp; he could hardly run and only with considerable difficulty.

"I've been in prison," he volunteered. "Twenty days." I expressed surprise on my face. I think he was very sensitive about his physical disability. He then spoke with an intensity and force that made me feel slightly embarrassed.

"They had a demonstration at one end of the village. At the time I was working in my garden." I remembered now, he was a keen gardener and kept a fine aviary.

"My house was not near the demonstration, but the soldiers chased the young men and boys through the village. The young men evading the troops rushed off the road into my garden. Tear gas was fired close to where I was working. I struggled to get away and was caught by the soldiers."

"You were throwing stones, they said. I told them that I wasn't, I was working in my garden. How could I have got from one end of the village to the other with this leg, I told them. Then they accused me of putting stones on the road. I denied this, but they insisted I had. I told them heatedly that I was only half a man and could not have done it in the time they claimed. You come with us , was their answer. I was shoved into the truck. God will be my witness I shouted. They laughed, let him, they cried." So he was imprisoned in the detention centre south of Hebron. All the other young men had apparently escaped.

He half turned as if to go, and his fierce eyes met mine. He had not many friends in the University, I wondered what sort of hell he went through in prison.

"You wont forget to tell them will you?" he said, with determination. He left the closed steel gates and paced, in his awkward manner, the empty street. He had come all the way from a village the other side of Hebron. I shouted after him, "No, I won't forget to tell them." I felt bad about it and my lack of sensitivity. The frustration of it all: I could at least have invited him to the house for some refreshment and a chat instead of standing in the cold street. But then, I ran the risk of seeing him in prison again.

"It's all planned," explained Alfred, in an excited voice. He was leaning on his desk in a small office in his warehouse, looking inspired and authoritative.

"You mean the Intifada?" I queried, with a hint of incredulity. He gave me a look, as if to say, I doubted his words. Alfred had worked for the British army during the Mandate days. He was an intelligent man, he now owned a small business which, like many in Bethlehem, ran the risk of bankruptcy as the Intifada continued.

"You see," he explained conspiratorially, the Americans, the British and the Jordanians planned the Intifada." I must have blinked again.

"Of course they started it! They planned to frighten the intransigent Israeli government. Force them to become more flexible." "That's daring," I muttered half under my breath.

"Look, it's obvious. You just have to watch, who goes where and who meets whom. Wasn't King Hussein in London with Mrs Thatcher? Wasn't Mr Shultz there too!" Alfred then launched into his theme, proving beyond doubt, the credibility of his reasoning. He interpreted the complexities of the international scene; all the strands worked towards his thesis in a conclusive and tidy fashion.

Listening, it reminded me of remarks Glubb Pasha made about the Arabs in one of his books about the Middle East. The British Foreign Office, or the then Colonial Office, had perpetrated yet another policy blunder in the Middle East. The Arabs could never recognise the sheer simplicity of what had merely been a mistake. Instead they built around the incident complex and involved interpretations giving credit to the British for sheer devilry and Machiavellian machinations, when meer folly was nearer the truth.

"Of course, King Hussein will abdicate," he cried, rising, as if he was embarking on his peroration, and I slightly fearful that I had missed the meaty arguments that logically drove him to this statement. "Why should he?" I interjected with a certain timerity. A momentary flash of pity (or was it exasperation) crossed his genial face. I was obviously proving a slow pupil in the art of politics and the intricacies of the Middle East. "He's a millionaire. He's a sick man. When there is a Palestinian state that is democratic, do you think he will survive in Jordan where 70 percent of the people are Palestinians?"

I left, my mind buzzing and slightly befuddled . I wanted to dismiss all of what I had heard. And yet, I had to remind myself, this was a land of unpredictability. May be there was some element of truth in part of his dissertation.

◆   ◆

The Israeli soldiers had sprayed a graffiti on the walls of the local convent school. It was in bad taste and gave offence. "Sex lessons given here, first lesson free." The bright red letters could hardly be missed by the children as they entered the school. Whether the troops did it through boredom or in a spirit of frustration, I don't know. Perhaps it was further evidence of an individualism creeping into the way in which the occupying troops interpreted their orders or just thoughtless young men having some fun. In an indirect way it provided us with some light humour.

One of the sisters from the convent and her close friend, Miss Bie, both friends and colleagues in the University, were guests at our residence and were relaxing after dinner around the fire. As I said, we were all close friends. I decided to have some mischief. Perhaps it was the bonhomie that develops after a good meal.

"Well sister," I said. "How are your sex lessons progressing?" Everyone was aware of the red graffiti. Like lightening, and in her appealing French-English, Miss Bie lightly interjected. "She goes, but she doesn't understand".

Everyone howled with laughter. We need that here.

XXIII / THE ALMOND BLOSSOMS ARE OUT NOW IN BETHLEHEM

We sang German ballads and some Simon and Garfunkel almost to midnight. German helpers at the Benedictine monastery at Tabghar, a sprinkling of scripture scholars and theologians from the Dormitian Abbey, Jerusalem, gathered round the timber fire. Dare I say, we saw a million stars in the clear blackness above. Across the unseen horizon glimmered the varied lights of Tiberias. The Horns of Hattin loomed menacing, dark cliffs of death for the travelling crusaders, eight hundred years ago. How well the Germans sing; harmonies flow naturally, guitars sprung rhythms, gentle cadences across the waters of the Sea of Galilee. I felt as though, I was released from prison, such was the relief of leaving the tensions of Bethlehem and the Intifada. So we celebrated Saturday evening after vespers; we broke bread at Tabghar.

I left Bethlehem the day before just as another three day strike was declared. As I travelled from the West Bank the rumour quickly spread that a young man from the nearby village of Ubeidiya had died from earlier injuries sustained during the uprising. We had just finished a series of strikes. One three day episode was in protest at the heavy taxation imposed on the pharmacies. One particular pharmacy which could not pay the heavy tax of 150,000 shekels (£50,000) had its entire drug stock, car and television confiscated. The ruthless economic campaign to subdue the Palestinians continues. Troops are everywhere checking in the streets with the military central computer if individuals have paid their taxes. Identity cards, cars, durable goods from peoples' homes are taken if taxes are in arrears. And yet, inspite of all, spring has come, the almond trees are in blossom.

The Egged bus to Tiberias was crowded. Midday, Friday, meant the Israelis were taking their last opportunities to travel before the Shabbat. The bus was full of young soldiers, the passageway made virtually impassable by piles of kit bags. The young men in khaki were exhausted, leaning and lolling their weary bodies against anything that would support their sleep. Where were these soldiers coming from? Perhaps night manoeuvres in the desert or patrols on the West Bank or policing the hell hole of Gaza? The bus radio blared. The news announced the deaths of two Palestinians; there were tired cheers. The young soldier beside me collapsed into sleep again, his automatic weapon pressed against my thigh. Was it the heat of Jericho and the Jordan valley that caused my mind to wander and recall the lines of an Irish poet friend? An Irish man, with gentle passion, will understand the plight of Palestinians.

Checkpoint "Listen, soldier, three days in a row
       you've made me stop, checked my ID.
       I'm not the one who'll bring you woe.
       I've seen your enemy at work,
       kids out of school, whooping it up,
       volleying stones against your shields.
       They move so fast it's laser beams
       you'd need, not guns, not CS gas.
       Even when your aim is true they rise
       again, like Christ. Reflect on Him.
       How can you put them down when death
       authenticates their final throw?

My brief release from the confinement of the West Bank reminded me of Doctor Isaac Jad's termination of his detention from prison and his sixth month experience there. Ansar 3 is located in the flat barren Negev Desert. It is not only distant from the green completeness of the Sea of Galilee but a total antithesis to the freedom experienced here. Doctor Isaac Jad, a Greek Orthodox Christian, a member of the Bethlehem University staff, suffered administrative detention for nearly six months in Ansar 3. He was arrested back in July 1988. His imprisonment was purely a measure, like many of the administrative detention arrests, to control the various forms of leadership during the Intifada. His crime, as a trained biologist, was to encourage self reliance in the form of crop growing and animal husbandry in his town of Beit Sahour

His story has many of the characteristics of the 4000 other Palestinians who were summarily arrested without trial for six months by military commanders in the occupied territories. He was arrested in his home at 4.00 a.m. on 8th July in front of his family. He spent three days in the cells at the Military Governor's headquarters in Bethlehem. Two of these days were in a cage 1 meter by 2 meters. The cage was covered by a blanket, which soldiers passing in the corridor, raised to gaze at him and abuse him. The summer heat, mosquitoes, flies, appalling food, which he refused to eat, and the general filth and darkness, made this the worst part of his experience.

Most inmates of Asnar 3 experienced a similar transfer to Doctor Jad's. He was moved to Dahriyyeh where he was held for three weeks before transfer to the Negev, Ansar 3. Travel on the buses was undertaken in an unpleasant way. They were handcuffed and blindfolded and forced to bow their heads. On Doctor Jad's transfer from Bethlehem to Dahriyyeh they were continually punched and beaten by a soldier who walked up and down the aisle of the bus. The small rooms in Dahriyyeh, which were generally no more than 5 meters long and 3 meters wide, held as many as twenty eight men in each. A single bucket of water served all their requirements for washing and refreshment which was filled twice a day. The toilet was one bucket in the corner of the crowded room. The heat and stench was almost unbearable. There was no change of clothing, no washing or shaving equipment and Doctor Jad said he left the room three times during the three weeks for a rapid shower without any towels. They ate their food with dirty hands. The only time Doctor Jad's wife saw him was in this state at Dahriyyeh. She was horrified at his appearance and hardly recognized him.

The attitude of the Israelis towards prisoners in Dahriyyeh was further aggravated by the constant beatings, particularly when interrogations were taking place. Beatings with hands, kicking, the use of electric shocks on the body and isolation in a steel cabinet for three days were some of the methods applied. Al-Haq, Law in the Service of Man, has a document entitled, "Dahriyyeh, Centre of Punishment," gives a detailed report on the situation. Military police, and not Prison Authority officers, ran the prisons and were in charge of the manner in which the prisoners were treated. Al-Haq, an organisation of lawyers, were concerned that the treatment of Palestinians in the prisons would drive even more men to extremism and perpetuate the problems.

Ansar 3 is located in the wilderness of the Negev desert near some military camps. The prison is divided into three compounds; Doctor Jad was in compound A. Each compound had five sections, each up to about 224 men. In every section were eight tents each housing up to 28 men. Here there were no interrogations and prisoners generally managed to avoid contact with the Israelis particularly after the disturbing events earlier in August 1988, when two prisoners were shot and several wounded inside the compound. Apart from the roll calls, the prisoners spent much of their day with their own organized activities between frugal meals. Lessons in languages (Doctor Jad learnt Hebrew in prison) and other subjects filled the mornings. There were no family visits and lawyers were unable to help much as they could only see their clients for a few minutes.

During Doctor Jad's stay in Ansar 3 he carried out an economic and sociological survey with 180 men out of 204 in his section. Though the survey was from one section and necessarily has the limitations of a sample study, some of the results are informative. First the geographical distribution of prisoners indicated they were from all over the West Bank except for the men from Gaza, who had their own compound, and the men from East Jerusalem, who were detained elsewhere. There were a higher percentage of men from the villages and from the camps. The number of men from Jenin and Jericho were high compared proportionally with the total population figures of the towns on the West Bank.

Age distribution indicated a total range from 21 to 56 years with the average coming to 26.4 years. About 60 percent of all the detainees were between the ages of 21 and 29 years of age while the percentage of this age group amongst all Palestinian men is 47 percent Two thirds of the detainees had experienced secondary schooling, only four could be considered illiterate, 20 had B.Sc. or B.A. degrees, two had masters degrees and two had doctorates. Doctor Jad was keen to point out that those men that had not received much of a formal education and who had been in prison for many years were widely read, spoke at least three languages and had a wide and wise experience of life.

Employment and economic backgrounds represented a wide spectrum of the West Bank labour force ranging from academicians to unskilled labourers. There were 22 merchants, 39 skilled technicians, 11 public employers, teachers, a lawyer, a medical doctor and a dentist, 8 farmers, 21 students, and 53 unskilled workers. Of the 180 interviewed, 136 owned their own houses and more than 50% of the sample own agricultural land. The average monthly income for the group was 132 Jordanian dinars. One dinar at present, with the recent fall in the value of the currency, has a value equal to two American dollars.

The sociological background showed 76 married, 14 engaged, and 90 bachelors. The average size family among the detainees was 6.8 per family. Also interesting, and showing the extent of the arrests, was the analysis of the number of times individuals had been arrested. Only for 38 of the detainees was this the first time and 19 others were detained only during the uprising. There were 43 men who had another member of their immediate family in detention and 6 who had more than one. Most of the men had been arrested in their homes but 6, 21 and 8 were arrested from their work, in the street and at army road blocks respectively. Boredom was the hardest issue for the first-time detainees while lack of family visits was a crucial concern for those that had been detained before. Food and water, environmental conditions and hygiene and cleanliness were important but less pressing.

Doctor Jad concludes that this survey completed in October 1988, in one section of Ansar 3, of men who are detained but not convicted or charged, shows how wide the movement for freedom is on the West Bank and Gaza. Nearly all sectors of the community have been targeted for this kind of preventative detention which may very well support the thesis that the Intifada is a people led activity.

At the time of writing there are far fewer administrative detainees in Ansar 3. However, that is not to say that it is only partially occupied. Today it is packed with over 5000 prisoners of various categories from the uprising. Yesterday, another one of our teaching staff at Bethlehem University was released. His only crime was organizing reading lessons for small children when the schools were closed. His six months in Ansar 3 were through the winter which was often wet, even in the desert. Apparently, the only dry place was on his raised mattress; mud and water were everywhere and the cold intense, particularly at night. There was great rejoicing in his family and town last night as I returned from the Sea of Galilee.

I said to the almond tree,
"Sister, speak to me of God."
And the almond tree blossomed.

XXIV / TO THINK THE UNTHINKABLE

I was floating in a very relaxed manner on my back in the Dead Sea. A day
trip to the Jordan Valley with my two sisters had taken us to the customary
bathing experience in the Dead Sea. It was pleasantly warm at Ein Gedi and
restful after seeing Qumran and Masada in the heat. I was so preoccupied
attempting to balance some large stones on my stomach, in order to emphasize
the buoyancy of the salt water that it was only later that I noticed my sisters
were in earnest conversation with another woman. Eventually I was drawn into
the conversation with her as my sisters left the water to get showered and
changed.

"You're an Israeli, aren't you?" she queried. "No," I said, " I come from
near London, I'm English." I was rather well tanned at the time, my sisters were
quite pale having endured the uncertainties of the English winter and spring.
The woman was about forty, She was anxious to talk. She was born in Russia,
in Leningrad. Both she and her husband were Jews; he was a physics professor
at Leningrad University. Six years ago they planned and received permission
to leave Russia and with their two daughters settle in Israel. They wanted to
leave the unjust situation and enjoy a homeland and freedom in a democratic
state. I asked where she had learnt her English; she spoke so competently. "I
studied English and English literature for my degree in Leningrad University,"
she assured me. Her family was at the airport ready to board the plane to come
to Israel when the Russian police arrested her husband. If I recall correctly,
she said, the only explanation given, required him to stay, since he was a scientist
and essential to the needs of the state. The mother and two daughters continued
their journey to Israel without the husband. I was quite shocked to discover
that she had not seen or heard of her husband since. She had lived in Israel
for six years and no communication, after numerous attempts, had not succeed-
ed in contacting her husband.

She continued to tell me how happy and relieved she was to be an Israeli
citizen, how well she was received and catered for. She was provided with an
apartment in Gilo, given lessons in Hebrew, trained as a teacher and now employed in the Israeli educational system. Both her daughters had settled well,

knew the language and received a good schooling. I think one of them was at the Hebrew University.

It was during our conversation that an Arab family, mother, father and three children came down to the waters' edge. Having seen them, she turned to me quite in anger. "Why are those people allowed here!" there was fear and venom in her voice. I was quite shaken by the tone and intensity of the hostility. The profound irony of the situation was so apparent.

In writing these short stories I have tried to write about human beings, ordinary folk, mothers, fathers, students, children, families. My presence among the Palestinians demonstrated the genuine humanness and essential goodness of most with whom I came in contact. I am sure, had I been in Israel living with and knowing Israeli families and sharing their friendship, it would be the same. I cherish the fleeting and passing encounters I have had with Jewish students on an Egged bus travelling down to Eilat, of dinner one evening with undergraduates form Hebrew University, of the warm welcome, concern and help from members of the Hebrew University staff and of friends who looked after me once in Eilat. To walk the corridors of the Hebrew University was an experience far closer to my culture; though the geography and faces were a little different, the atmosphere reminded me of Queen Mary College, London. And yet, I felt cut off in so many ways because of the situation here. Much of my contact with Israel was through the military, security officials, particularly at airports, who did not look on me kindly; sometimes the treatment was unsympathetic and unnecessarily aggressive and at times demeaning.

How are conflicts resolved? Historians, it seems to me, have spent far more time on analysing how wars begin rather than concern for how they end and how the peace is organised. I spent part of last summer on a course called Conflict-Resolution. The no-fault negotiating formula was used by individuals in conflict by listening and identifying the specific behaviours of each other, sharing assumptions about the possible causes of their conflict, saying how they feel emotionally about the situation, explaining their needs and saying what they wanted. These were stages in a process towards resolution of differences. The stages in this dynamic, however, depended on the form of thinking and relating that the individuals had reached. The capacity for individuals to negotiate varied in time and with their environment, I often wondered where whole nations and large groups would be if they utilized this methodology. I could not help thinking that in the Arab-Israeli conflict the form of thinking and relating was pre-rational, subject to fear, blocking out the needs of others, based on power and force requiring essential security and motivated to avoid punishment. With this level of thinking only the first stages of conflict resolution can be attempted. Much has yet to be accomplished to change the level of reasoning and yet I detect a measure of good will among people on both sides. What is needed and that is sadly lacking, is quality leadership and statemanship. For the Israelis, who are in power, a statemanship of moderation. For the Arabs, a leadership which will accept compromise, disown terrorism, recognize Israelis' right to exist and to attempt to unify the often disparate individualism of Palestinians.

I have attempted to describe, as a bystander, some of the events and faces of Palestinians before and during the Intifada. In the day to day activities, sometimes chaos, disorder and tragedies there is a risk of losing sight of the fundamental issue which had generated the uprising. For me the crucial consideration is the occupation of the West Bank and Gaza for over twenty years, surely one of the longest military occupations in modern times, against the legitimate rights of the people there. Abba Eban in the Jerusalem Post for November 11th 1988, says the problem will not go away. After the Israeli elections, where some commentators speculate the results have dealt a death-blow to the prospect of land for peace, Abba Eban, claims this is a "rash and superficial appraisal." He utilises the parallel of Israelis denying Newton's Law of Gravitation. They called for the law's abolition but "apples detached from trees would continue to move downward and would not leap joyously toward the sky."

As I write this towards the end of February 1989, much has happened on the international scene. The Palestinian National Conference has taken place. A Palestinian state declared. The Declaration document appears to be an impressive statement. There will be, its formulators hope, a secular state with a democratic government, with all the freedoms that entails: free elections, a free press, freedom of religion and equality of the sexes. The diplomatic campaign of the PLO certainly gained ground towards a peaceful solution of the immense problems here. The drama surrounding Schultz's refusal to allow Arafat to speak at the UN in New York, the subsequent transfer of the assembly to Geneva and the final, at last, begrudging acceptance of the Americans to talk with the PLO. It was Talleyrand, who said somewhere, that statesmanship often consists of "cooperating with the inevitable."

Sadly, and demonstrating the real fears that Israel has, its present leaders have gone on the offensive diplomatically to prevent talks taking place. T.S. Eliot claimed that mankind cannot stand too much reality but surely there must be a limit to the intransigency of Israel's leaders. It would seem that to negotiate now for them, would mean, to negotiate from strength.

It was Landrum Bolling, the director of the Tantur Institute and unofficial go-between for various leaders in the Middle East who asked Arafat, in one of his meetings with him, what would a Palestinian state offer its people. Arafat said it would not offer them very much in itself. There would, he said, be a piece of ground where they could be buried, where they could retire. It is true that the West Bank and Gaza, once they are independent, offer only a limited economic base on which to build. Any reading of Doctor Meron Benvenisti's reports from the West Bank Data Base Project demonstrate, even without all the necessary data, indicates the poverty of the West Bank and Gaza Strip. Under both Jordanian and Israeli administrations, military, political and economic oppression has further weakened the economy and resources of the West Bank and Gaza.

Yet in spite of these weaknesses the Palestinian will be free again: free to move, to think, to fly a flag, to carry a Palestinian passport, free to express ideas and to communicate them within a Palestinian culture and identity. I will always remember, when I asked one of my Palestinian students when I first arrived in this land and was fairly uninformed, what was her great wish or dream. "Let us be free," she said.

The concept of the Nation State has provided many advantages for the self expression and determination of people who believed in themselves and who were convinced of their own identity, way of life, culture and values. Yet the whole concept, after two world wars and an increasingly divided and dangerous world with an unjust distribution of wealth and an increasing fragile environment and depleted resources, is called into question. Lynn Miller, in his book "Global Order" argues a powerful case for the declining usefulness of the Westphalian ideal. Sovereign nation states, by definition and nature, promote self interest, oppose competing powers in order to protect their people. No state is really responsible for another; at worst nationalism is the anarchy of the survival of the fittest. People and states become inseparable. Would a new Palestinian State, run on these lines, provide a peaceful geopolitical environment for the future?

Some years ago Johaun Baptist Metz wrote: "We Christians can never again go back behind Auschwitz: to go beyond Auschwitz, if we see clearly, is impossible for us by ourselves. It is possible only together with the victims of Auschwitz." For this German Catholic theologian, Christians not only must recognize how their power and triumphalism persecuted the Jews over the centuries but in this new awareness should embrace their once Jewish victims. Doctor Marc Ellis, a Jewish theologian, applying the same ideal to the Jewish empowerment after the Holocaust, sees a Jewish world community of power and confidence expressing its nationhood in the state of Israel. But like Christians, in their relationship with the Jews in the past, they are confident in the justice and rightness of their empowerment, becoming blind to and finding it almost impossible to admit to their own complicity in the suppression of the Palestinian people. Doctor Ellis argues, that for a lasting Middle East Settlement, particularly between the Jew and Arab, there must be a deep reconciliation. For the Jewish community around the world and in Israel, they cannot be liberated without the liberation of the Palestinian people. He in fact calls for a new Jewish Liberation Theology.

Somehow, sometime, these highly gifted people who have lived and worked in this Golden Crescent, belong to each other and must get along together. I would like to think, think the unthinkable, that while these people remain autonomous, some political instrument will be created to find a confederal arrangement with Israel and Jordan and the tiny Palestinian State nestled between them. Only a liberating revision of the Holocaust theology could make this possible from the Israeli side. Recently, when Michael Sabbah, the Palestinian Latin Patriarch, when challenged about this stand on the Palestinian issues replied "I am a Palestinian; but if the Israelis were oppressed, I would be on their side and speak out for them."

Elie Weisel says in "The Gates of the Forest": "God made man because he loves stories." I have told mine living among the Palestinians. How often we turn both our pain and ecstasy into narrative. Often my experiences and relationships are found in an environment that expresses pain. But if what I believed elaborates on what feels to me to be profoundly true, though not always clearly demonstrable, I want to believe in better things. There are still enough good people who have values and convictions with both the Israelis and the Palestinians. May they listen to each other. May there be a second coming to Bethlehem, not W.B. Yeat's beast, but good news, for all.

Part 3

Christmas 1989
to
Easter 1991

CHAPTER XXV / BEIT SAHOUR AGAIN

"How was your trip?" they asked. "We haven't seen you in a long time!" In September 1989 I returned to Bethlehem for the third time from my summer work in Seattle University. "How is it?" continued my student friends. "Do the foreign newspapers say what is going on here?" I was loath to tell them that other news filled the world's press and media. I told them there was a cartoon in a Seattle newspaper that showed a woman reading a paper and telling her husband: "More students killed!" It was during the momentous and tragic events in China. The husband questioned: "Students in Tianaman Square?" "No!" came the firm retort. "Students on the West Bank and Gaza!"

The day before, I had been driven back to the University on the return journey from the airport. As we turned into Fréres Street my driver confrere must have seen my face drop. I caught a glimpse of the University tennis courts. "They are not in use," he said. Clearly the tennis courts were unplayable. Local Palestine youths had vandalized the tennis courts and no tennis was played on them for months. I felt depressed; my one opportunity for recreation had been destroyed. Apparently the young men objected to the foreigners enjoying themselves on the courts. I half smiled to myself when I recalled having a tough time leaving Israel with an arrogant young man in Israeli security at the airport last May. "Why are you carrying a tennis racket?" he demanded with some menace. "I play," I answered. "There are no tennis courts in Bethlehem!" he insisted, just as earlier he made it quite clear that Palestine did not exist and the State of Israel extended from the Mediterranean to the river Jordan. At the time I was quietly amused for tennis courts did exist in Bethlehem, tucked away on the University campus, and I was equally sure that Israel's undefined boundaries did not extend to the river Jordan.

Conversation at dinner in the brothers' community that evening was studded with items that were meant to "fill me in" on the current situation in Bethlehem. "And you know my room!" one vociferous New Yorker declared, as though it had only happened yesterday. "A bullet smashed my window, a rubber bullet from 200 yards away and another shattered the glass on the registrar's notice board." Apparently the brothers were on the verandah which overlooks the valley when a disturbance took place in Star Street. All they could remember were the loud bangs and the shattering of glass above their heads. I was shown the new rubber bullets; they were collected from around the house. They were new to me and very different from those in use last May. They were quite heavy ball bearings with a very thin coating of rubber fired 6 at a time. It seemed to me they would be lethal from a range of 100 yards and had the added danger of bouncing off walls and surfaces.

The conversation then turned to the dramatic events in the neighbouring village of Beit Sahour. "You recall our car mechanic who services the University transport? He lost most of the equipment in his garage and all of the valuable items from his house. There's a tax war going on. It started just before you returned on 19th September." I remembered the raids made on the pharmacists in both Bethlehen and Beit Sahour. My Palestinian tennis partner ran a pharmacy in Beit Sahour. I knew something about it as he had talked to me about it last May.

Later in the week I met teaching staff and friends from Beit Sahour. Doctor Jad and Claudette gave me further details of what is now a well documented account of the tax revolt in Beit Sahour.

"It's almost unbelievable," one friend said. " They are wiping out forty years of hard work building up commerce and industry. Our Christian town, Beit Sahour, has been here for over four hundred years. Now they are trying to force us out." Sealed off and under continuous curfew the Israeli army with tax collectors were systematically destroying the economic life of the town. "It started with the pharmacies, then the shops, then the factories and now it is the homes. Mass raids attempt to force the population to pay the unjust taxes. We are all in the same boat. There is no choice. The pharmacies were given arbitary figures between 20 and 60 thousand dollars to pay. Compound fines are then added so that the figure demanded is quite incredible."

"Why aren't you paying the taxes?"I asked a Beit Sahour friend. "First," he said quite emphatically, "we believe there should be no taxation without representation." The Jerusalem Post and American national papers later carried articles with titles reminiscent of the tax revolt in America. The phrase, "Beit Sahour tea party," was fast becoming a slogan. He went on to claim that the taxes were illegal. Under the Geneva Convention taxes such as the Israeli (VAT), imposed in 1976 by the occupying power, had no legal basis. The Israeli army were mobilised to collect these taxes in a most arbitary manner. It was then pointed out that those taxes collected, were by international law, to be spent on the services of the land under occupation. The Israelis did not publish accounts of taxes collected nor did they show how the monies raised were spent. It was abundantly clear to any casual observer, looking at the services and other facilities in the area that there was a vast difference between what was spent on these items in Israel and what was allocated for the same services on the West Bank and the Gaza Strip. "Nobody here has a pension from the state or social security. Just look at the state of the roads and the schools!" my friend complained.

During the weeks that followed the people of Beit Sahour remained steadfast. Each day the Israeli response became more and more severe. A full scale military operation was mounted. After the total curfew of five days from 19th to 24th September, a nightly curfew, from 5.00pm to 5.00am was extended for several weeks. Only people from Beit Sahour could get in or out. Most of the foreign consuls, the different Christian Patriarchs and the press attempted to get in but were turned back. On Friday 27th October I saw the convoy of cars with the Patriarchs stopped by military road blocks near Tantur. Similar treatment was accorded to the various consuls on other occasions. The British Consul General finally drove his private Land Rover round some tracks at the back of Beit Sahour and to the embarrassment of the military witnessed some of the brutality that accompanied the tax raids at first hand.

It was Claudette who told me about the restrictions on food. All shops in Beit Sahour were closed, food could only be obtained from outside the town. Soldiers were searching every car and person entering the town. In some cases, if they considered they were carrying more food than the individual soldier felt necessary, the food was crushed underfoot on the spot. So serious became the shortages of basic foods that various agencies were attempting to smuggle much needed foodstuffs into the town. Various shops, factories and organizations were hiding the stocks of goods and furnishings in an attempt to avoid confiscation by the tax officers.

Once the town was thoroughly sealed off the work of pillage could commence. Six hundred tax refusers were targetted in the campaign. Several weeks later 150 inhabitants were arrested, approximately 80 were held as political detainees and 55 were sentenced to 5 to 6 months of imprisonment in addition to having their property confiscated. The very nature of the military seige makes it difficult to accurately evaluate the value of the property lost. It is estimated by some observers however that $3,000,000 worth of property and goods were lost. These were stored in large warehouses at Ben Gurion airport awaiting an auction that the government would organize for Israeli purchasers.

Weeks later when I visited a student's home he and his father invited me to see their cedar wood workshop. They pointed out to me the steel stumps of the legs on which the expensive machine lathes were mounted. Troops had invaded the premises with the tax officers, trucks drew up outside, the place was surrounded by soldiers. Army engineers then brought in their cutting equipment; $8,000 worth of machinery was loaded into the trucks and driven away. Years of saving and hard work and the opportunity to earn a living were destroyed within half an hour. Neither the student or his father complained of brutality. Elsewhere this was not the case.

Typical of the hundreds of raids on homes was one of the first carried out on 19th September 1989. At 9.00am., soldiers arrived at the shop of Mr. George Beshara Mas'ad. They arrested his son, Beshara, and informed him that he would remain in their custody until his father paid his taxes. At 2.30pm. a group of approximately 50 went to Mr. George Mas'ad's house. Finding themselves unable to force their way indoors, the soldiers went upstairs to the house of his brother where they were let in by the latter's mother and wife. His brother's mother was in her late sixties, she protested that the soldiers were in the wrong house. The soldiers threw her on the floor where she suffered a "heart blockage" induced by the stress and the violent physical treatment. When her daughter in law attempted to use the telephone to get a doctor a soldier ripped the telephone off the wall. Both were subsequently locked into a room while the soldiers removed sofas, carpets, a television and a guitar from the house. A military doctor was finally called who stated that the elderly woman had suffered a minor heart attack. No ambulance was called. It was only when the soldiers left that an ambulance was finally summoned and she was admitted into the intensive care unit of the Makassed hospital in East Jerusalem.

Frequent beatings, humiliations, arrests and inhuman treatment by the Israeli army and tax officials on the people of Beit Sahour did not break their spirit. Other more mean methods were used to subjugate the people. The tax collectors made use of very small children to circumvent their parents. In one house I was told how the tax collectors would ask a four year old whether the two televisions in the house belonged to tnem. The unsuspecting infant would say that one of the televisions belonged to their neighbours; it would be promptly taken away.

On the 30th of October 1989 the Military authorities announced that they were ending their tax collection campaign. The people of Beit Sahour had not given way. On the 5th of November at 10.00am in the Roman Catholic Church of Beit Sahour, Christian, Moslem and Jewish leaders from Palestine, Israel and abroad, as well as representatives from the international community, members of the Knesset (the Israeli parliament) and Palestinians and Israelis from the Peace movement prayed for peace and for freedom. The special purpose of their prayers was to tell the Israeli military authorities and the world that they were determined to have their freedom and independence and that there should be peace between Israelis and Palestinians. It was good to see that the people of Beit Sahour could at last meet their spiritual leaders, the Patriarchs, who were earlier prevented from seeing their spiritual flocks as well as from praying in their churches.

Though it is true that the people of Beit Sahour won their battle with the tax collectors, it was nevertheless a victory at great personal, economic and social cost. No one, as far as I know, gave way, though many secret attempts were made to bribe or intimidate people into submission. I discovered that there was a spectrum of different views on the tax revolt amongst the people of Beit Sahour. Some had second thoughts and at the time felt that years of initiative and industry had been destroyed. They considered the tax war a mistake because of the probability that the Intifada would drag on forever. To use this weapon of tax evasion, unless all Palestinians acted together in coordination, invited severe hardships on their well knit and active community.

Many Beit Sahour inhabitants believe otherwise. They argue that the tax revolt came at a crucial time when the Intifada was lagging in its momentum. They also claim that Beit Sahour was a test case which severely embarrassed the Military Government. Furthermore, had it not been for the dramatic events in Eastern Europe and in Russia which shifted the attention of the world's political leaders away from the Middle East, a breakthrough may well have been made. How ironic that now when the attention of the international community has finally shifted back to the Middle East (following Iraq's invasion of Kuwait) the Palestinians should once again be the losers. The Palestinians who wholeheartedly supported the tax strike also point to the genuine recovery in the Beit Sahour economy which has occurred since the end of the strike and that at least some of the monies lost were replaced by funds from outside. The industries of the town, though they have not fully recovered, are at least operating again.

Despite their occasional successes and their ever present hardships, most Palestinians now realize that the uprising may well be a long drawn out battle in which tax evasion will from time to time play a prominent role.

XXVI / VOICES FROM BETHLEHEM: CHRISTMAS 1989

Father George Abu Khazen, a Lebanese Franciscan, is the Catholic parish priest for the town of Bethlehem. You find your way to his offices up the stairway from the cloister located in front of the church of St. Catherines which adjoins the Nativity.

"You are living in Bethlehem, you know what Christmas means to the Christians in Bethlehem," he said, as we sat down in his office sipping Arabic coffee out of the customary small cups. "We still celebrate the feast religiously, but it is no longer a social or civil feast or occasion. We feel we cannot celebrate an exterior feast. We have many young people in prison at the present time."

"How many?" I asked.

"I think about sixty." He went on to say that many of the young men from the parish had been affected this way and so naturally their families felt solidarity with them. "You know," he continued, "even Abu Elias, our porter here, he has had at one time all three of his sons in prison. He still has one there."

"Talking about the young men, Abuna, have many left to go abroad?"

"Ninety young people left in 1988. Almost the same number this year, but I have to know the exact number, when we bless each of the families' houses, I will know. We have, for example, a widow who now lives alone, all her sons, three of them, have gone outside. This is a serious loss to our parish of four thousand, two hundred people."

"Isn't there a particular irony of the loss of unborn babies in Bethlehem too?" I inquired.

"In my parish," he said with feeling, "I have examples of mother's having miscarriages."

"Because of tear gas?" I ventured.

"Yes because of tear gas, and we have two families, who left their own houses to go to another place in order to have the babies, because of the danger in Wadi Ma'ali and Madbasseh, you know. Parents, too, who wish to have another child, hesitate to do so now."

The telephone rang. Everything with a bell, it seems, in this part of the world, rings extra loudly. Father George answered in arabic. Later there were other telephone calls: in one he talked in Italian, in the other in French. I was somewhat embarrassed when he apologised for what he considered his weak English.

"You know," he explained, "the people are becoming more and more depressed and some are loosing, how do you say, their esperance?"

"Hope for the future," I intervened.

"Yes, much hope for the future," he affirmed. "they are becoming needy people, even and especially, the class moyen." He explained how the middleclass used to help the parish, the poor, society generally. "Really they suffer too with the poor. Bethlehem is not an agricultural or industrial town, it has services and some commerce. These are declining."

"Do the people have enough to eat?" I asked. He moved restlessly in his chair. "Not all the people have enough to eat," his tone of voice conveying his anxiety. "If they have enough to eat they can't buy clothes. Somebody who sells clothes and shoes also suffers. We have many such shops in Bethlehem." He went on as if to emphasize the point. "Many families have no fruit, no vegetables and no meat. It is a problem. Last year, you know, vegetables and fruit were plentiful and cheap. This year no! It is difficult. We have to help these families."

"Have any social changes taken place in the parish during the uprising?"

"Sure, sure," he laughed a little nervously. "Yes, Bethlehem is a conservative society, very conservative. It's the clan, you know, the families, that were the authority. How do you say?" He searched for the appropriate English. "The relationship was subordination, subordination to the father, and the father to the head of the clan. It was something positive, something negative. Many family problems could be solved by the clan. But now," he continued, "these structures are weakened because the young people have another mentality, another way of thinking. The young people accuse their parents of doing nothing to end the twenty-three years of military occupation and claim, that they, the young generation, are doing something. This new attitude will have repercussions in the families, the clans, in the schools, in the church, in everything."

"Bethlehem seems much quieter, the army appears to have greater control," I suggested rather tentatively.

"It's not quiet, it's not quiet!" he replied, almost heatedly.

"But I don't hear so much shooting, as in the past, from my room in the University," I argued.

"Sure, sure, the troops are everywhere on the roof tops and they don't mention the disturbances in the papers, they wish to keep Manger Road free for the pilgrims. But it is not so quiet elsewhere. Daily, we have something."

As I walked from the Nativity across Manger Square I met a former student from the University. She said she was now married. Her husband was a lecturer at the Gaza University. She then said he was arrested two days ago. And in Star Street, just before climbing the steps past the Suk, an Israeli jeep swerved round a corner. Green berets clambered out forcing a group of young Palestinian men and boys against a wall and taking their identity cards. Two boys were dragged and forced into the back of the jeep. It drove off at speed. People hardly stopped their shopping; they needed their food. Everything would be closed tomorrow and the West Bank sealed off. Saturday marked the end of the second year of the Intifada.

* * *

"For us, Christmas means occupation," Edmund Shahadeh, the director of The Bethlehem Arab Society for the Physically Handicapped and qualified physiotherapist declared, sitting behind his desk, in the centre where the Intifada seriously wounded are cared for. "Christmas is less and less important to us because at Christmas we feel more and more the occupation in Bethlehem. More soldiers, more security: this affects our daily lives directly. Some families exchange gifts. But this Christmas I doubt if there will be any gift changing. People have to buy the basic foods. Yesterday, our family were thinking what to do to make it a little symbolic. My brother-in-law decided to use sugar and rice as Christmas presents."

"How has the addition of the rehabilitation of the young Intifada wounded to your many other commitments affected your experience?" I asked.

"Patients coming here are severely wounded. They come here with a very low morale and psychology. They often come with the idea that life is over. They find it difficult to make a new life. Some of them were asking whether what happened to them was worthwhile. Especially young people, when they were in hospital, everybody was treating them like heroes. When they come to this place they find they have another kind of life. It is a life where they have to endeavour to become independent. Now we have with our other voluntary staff, a psychologist to help them through their problems. Gradually we have been able to change their attitudes and persuade them that life has to continue even when they are severely handicapped."

"What about when they leave the centre though?" I queried.

"There are financial and medical problems when they leave especially as many of them come from remote camps and villages. We are trying to develop out-reach programmes, but it is very difficult."

"The great majority of the injured are young?"

"Most of the injured," he explained, "were from the age of twelve to twenty five. We have, during the uprising, admitted one hundred and eighty young men and women and children; only four patients were above the age of forty. They have been injured by high velocity bullets, by plastic bullets and rubber bullets. The injuries result in paraplegics, quadraplegics, hemeplegics and amputations."

"But what about the young man I saw who was beaten?"

"Young people are beaten during the period of interrogation. What I hear and see is very upsetting and the boy you asked about enumerated to me the different kinds of sufferings he experienced to make him talk. He received heavy beatings, three men walked and jumped on his back and they used heavy traction on him. This resulted in his spine being dislocated and paralysis. He will be a paraplegic for life."

"The scale of the medical problems and the resulting suffering must be quite immense," I remarked.

"According to the published statistics and the data based project over 80,000 have suffered different kinds of injuries, from mild to severe, since the Intifada began. We have 135 to 140 who have lost one eye or two eyes. A similar number who have lost one or both testicles from beatings. We have 1,400, who have suffered compound fractures and need extensive treatment and rehabilitation. Then there are those that have become severely handicapped. So one can go on!"

"Tomorrow will be the anniversary, marking the end of the second year of the uprising. The cycle of the Intifada almost co-incides with Christmas," I suggested.

"Yes, Christmas," he sighed, "Ah, Christmas! It's something we hear and dream of. And not just the Christian community, but the Moslem community too; really we are longing to have a lasting peace!"

* * *

"I have mixed feelings about Christmas. There is a genuine sense of wonder in being in the locality of Bethlehem. There is however also a very strong dichotomy between the birth of the Prince of Peace, the Saviour, and life in a land where the occupiers keep the whole people under subjection. They subject them to their own whims. Even within the everyday realities of the occupation there is no consistency in how Palestinians will be treated. The land is ruled according to each soldier's or officials own indulgent wishes, with 1300 arbitrary military orders and changes–whether you meet this soldier or that soldier–it's quite unpredictable." Father Dennis Madden is a priest from the diocese of Baltimore and has a doctorate in psychology.

"What about your work with the Palestinians?" I asked.

"I'm at the Kalandia refugee camp nearly every day. One of the things we are doing is building a health centre there. This gives an opportunity to work with the people and to become part of their community. It's all Moslem–there are no Christians–in the camp."

"How do you find the peoples' morale there?"

"I think at the beginning of the Intifada there was a lot more euphoria, a lot more hope, that things were going to happen rapidly. And then there seemed to be a period of settling in, a kind of heaviness, the realization that this was going to be a long haul and that it will take a lot of steadfastness. But there is still a strong sense of determination, a strong will and real strength with the people to see this thing through. They are not going to turn back."

"And the stresses they are under?"

"One of the heavy burdens is not knowing what their individual futures will be, not having regular schooling, suffering from the inability to assemble freely and to play freely. The other day in the camp, for the first time, I saw some boys playing football, just for a short time, which they usually don't do. They were constantly looking over their shoulders to see if soldiers were coming. They are not even able to walk as a group, all these things we take for granted as part of our natural development, are being denied."

"And the long term effects of this?" I inquired.

"While they have a common enemy, they will manage, what happens afterwards, what kind of effect this deprivation will have, remains to be seen," he said in his quiet way.

"One of your aims was to get the Israelis involved with your work, was it not?"

"Yes, though the links are tenuous and often difficult we have had a success with Palestinian nurses from Gaza being trained in special skills at the Israeli Hadasseh hospital in Ein Karen. And then we have an Israeli woman helping in our health centre training Palestinians to treat others with sign language who have speech impediments. We have had joint meetings of Israeli and Palestinian psychologists and psychiatrists."

"What about the effects of this violence on the Israeli soldiers? Have you any comment?"

"I think we are beginning to see these already. This year there were 45 suicides amongst the Israeli soldiers, double the number from last year. Brutal activities brutalize people. How were these men, when they return to their homes, going to relate to their families, their children and their society? But the underlying thing–and this applies to both the Israelis and the Palestinians–is that we will not know the true cost of such brutality for a long time. I believe that where you have a group of basically moral people, who have found themselves doing immoral things, they are somehow going to have to justify this in their consciences. I suspect they will adapt with the usual methods that most of us do, with alcohol, drugs–any number of ways to deal with the pain." He paused in thought:

"Let me give just one simple example that happened at the camp the other day. An officer ordered a soldier to guard a fourteen year old Palestinian boy who had just been arrested. The soldier was carrying a heavy automatic weapon. The soldier complained that if the boy ran away he was forced to shoot him. "I can't do this. I have a son this age. Just the thought that I might have to shoot him. I can't do this!"

* * *

"Palestine was under occupation at Christ's birth, so I suppose there are some similarities." She started the conversation quietly but steadily raised her voice as she expressed her feelings. Jacqueline Sfeir has lived all her life in Bethlehem and now teaches at Bethlehem University. Her doctorate dealt with research into pre-schooling.

"Peace and love are hard to express when your home area becomes a military zone," she explained.

"But what about this Christmas during the Intifada? Is there any difference?" I inquired cautiously.

"Well this year holds much more hope because of the struggle, the uprising. We are fighting back for our rights to live. It is much more hopeful than before, at least, as I remember it from my childhood."

"You say there is hope, but isn't there suffering too? What sort of suffering do you see?"

"Well there are levels of suffering. The obvious, the more direct is the physical hurt. Then there is psychological hurt which follows from constantly being in confrontation with something. It could be anything, such as my experience of not being able to travel. I was supposed to be in Rome today. I wasn't able to go and this means that the work I have done on my papers since October, is wasted. This kind of frustration, this kind of hurt. The feeling of being incapable of doing anything, losing control, not being able to plan. This is another level of pain."

She went on to illustrate what Father Dennis Madden had emphasized earlier. She gave detailed examples of how at the lower end of the education system the Israeli policies were creating a generation of potentially illiterate young people. "The younger children I deal with are not aware of the kind of suffering they were going to experience," she said with growing intensity. These policies started before the Intifada. "As adults they will not be able to compete in the world of the 21st century. This is one of the hidden strategies of the Israelis."

"And the socialization that goes with schooling and the result of an education?" I submitted.

"This is it," she said with conviction. "It snowballs, it starts with education. It means what kind of profession: it means standard of living: it means the kind of family you can raise and their expectations. This is the hidden hurt of occupation policies. We have to fend for ourselves. So the only thing we grow up with, and this is the story of my childhood, is that we have no inheritance, no homeland, except our education. The Israelis know this. They know it is the basis for founding our nationhood."

"You seem to skim over the physical dangers, don't you?" I challenged. "Now there again I can touch on this at a first hand basis. Many think that the violence the children are exposed to will be detrimental. As a matter of fact children adapt and cope. So they recreate their childhood in any setting they find. They can create their childhood on a battlefield. This will be a battlefield childhood. Research shows that children have a much better chance of recuperating and dealing with violence if they have a home, if they have a family that is properly knit. This compensates for a lot of the struggles they go through. If they have nothing to go back to they create irreversible scars. Our children, have if anything, a home, a family. There is not only the nuclear family; every street, every home in their village or town is home. As one six year old, who had been involved in a confrontation with the soldiers said to me: he had friends in the walls, meaning he knew each wall, he felt much stronger than the soldiers."

* * *

Such were the conversations with friends and colleagues who work closely with Palestinians. It occurred to me that I had talked to them the day before the second anniversary of the beginning of the Intifada. The next day was December 9th. We were now about to commence the third cycle. We were also very close to Christmas. In my mind I had come to associate the early events of the uprising with Christmas. Bethlehem was the place where I lived, where I saw the suffering. Bethlehem, the place where Christ was born, Bethlehem the place where the good news was announced. What would the year 1990 bring? Already on the international scene great changes seemed to be taking place in Russia and in Eastern Europe. Would they have some impact on the situation in the Middle East? Would there be some hope that a solution be found to the tremendous problems facing the Palestinians and the Israelis? I now went to the Basilica of the Nativity on Christmas Day and prayed. It was a prayer of desperate faith for all the signs around me indicated a long, long haul, before good will and peace were established in this Holy Land.

XXVII / JERUSALEM EASTER 1990

My windows are not clean. The winter rains and the fine white dust from the Khamseen winds that blow cold off the desert have left an untidy brown film of dirt on the large panes. The magnificent panorama of the desert and the distant Mountains of Moab are obscured. Shall I clean the windows? If it rains again I would have wasted my time. I decided it was a time to clean. "Jam hiems transiit, Imber abiit et recessit." (Now the spring has come, the rains are over and gone).

For Easter 1990 something is happening which takes place only rarely. Together the Jews will celebrate the Pessah, the Passover of the Old Testament, during the Christians' Holy Week. This year too, the Christians of both the Eastern and Western Churches will celebrate the Risen Christ on the same day: a rare occurrence for the churches in Jerusalem. As I meet my Moslem students unofficially (our University has been closed for nearly two and a half years) they are tired and weak, not just because the strains of the Intifada, but because they are now well into the rigorous fasting of Ramadan in preparation for the great Moslem feast.

At a time of hope, of preparation for celebration and to commemorate deliverance and a break with the past Jerusalem is still a sign of contradiction. In Israel there is division and acrimony. The promise of the peace process is delayed as their government is in disarray. Fear and intransigence govern emotions. It is ironic that the Jews commemorate their deliverance across the Red Sea when today their military are building a large base at Dahlak on the islands off the coast of Ethiopia; they wish to control access to the Red Sea. In Jerusalem the Christians remain divided; there are five Christian patriarchs in Jerusalem. And daily, for Moslem and Christian Palestinians, the uprising, or Intifada, rages on, now into its 27th month. The Intifada, now overshadowed by momentous events elsewhere, continues to register protest against the injustices of 23 years occupation and the unlawful annexation of the Old City and East Jerusalem.

Jerusalem is just 20 minutes by car from Bethlehem. Occasionally we used say, "Let's go up to Jerusalem to the cinema!" For Bethlehem is functionally an outer suburb or satellite of the city. Today, Land Day, there will be Israeli soldiers and Border Police preventing Palestinians from going to Jerusalem. The West Bank and Gaza are cut off; many of the refugee camps will be under curfew. For the Palestinians Land Day is a day of protest. It commemorates not only the specific incidents in Galilee where Arabs were killed by Israelis when they opposed the confiscation of their land but the whole tragic injustice suffered by the Palestinians at the loss of all their lands. The narrow alleys and streets in Palestinian quarters of the Old City and the shops in the East Jerusalem will be deserted. Everywhere the towns and villages and camps on the West Bank, East Jerusalem and Gaza will be saturated with Israeli troops. Nothing moves below our house on Manger Road or on Star Street as I write this.

The political battle over the land is paralleled by the theological battle. Some Jews are claiming that there is theological basis to the annexation of territory. In theological discussions attempts are made to address the apparent Biblical claims that the land was God given to the Jews: claims justified after the event by the way the promise was described.

Recently, I challenged a Roman trained theologian confrere and colleague of mine. The "Land," the "Promised Land" has been the subject for great debate locally. He was struggling with the concepts implied in the ideas of a "Chosen People", "The Covenant" and "The Promised Land" and attempting to reconcile them with the realities and injustices that surrounded him each day. Why had he now clarified his position, I asked him? He no longer saw the "Land" as part of the "Covenant". Indeed, he had come to believe that if the Biblical texts covering these topics were treated in the same way as say the literary forms of the creation narrative in the Bible it would come to be seen that Moses'appropriation of other peoples land simply a smash and grab raid. He then commenced to quote from the relevant passages of St Paul and the letter to the Hebrews about the "New Covenant", the break from the old to the new which came when Christ died for all, tearing down the walls of hostility so that were no longer Jews and Gentiles, slaves and free, men and women.

I wasn't satisfied. He was a theologian trained to question, why the certainty now? It was, he said, his visits to the Makassad hospital in East Jerusalem that finally convinced him. In taking the young men, handicapped during the Intifada, to visit their friends at the hospital each Friday, he met a 13-year-old Palestinian boy called Mansour. He saw this little fellow as he lay against his pillow. As the boy struggled to move on the bed he noticed that both his legs had been blown off. One of his hands was missing and his face was blackened and pock marked. He was, also at that time, totally blind. Mansour was one of a family of nine who were seriously injured in Hebron. The Abu Sneineh family were together in their small court yard enjoying a meal in the sun when a Jewish settler lobbed a hand grenade over their wall. In his later visits to the hospital my theologian friend noticed that Mansour was darting about the place in a wheel chair, wore special glasses that gave him some vision and was the favourite of all the people in the ward.

Yet in spite of the hatred and violence, Jerusalem has witnessed the hunger for peace amongst Jews and Palestinians. It was in the New Year of 1990 that I joined in the human chain for peace that encircled the walls of the Old City of Jerusalem. I stood with the thousands and sang "shalom." I clasped the hands of a young Israeli student on my left and a Palestinian woman, wearing her traditional dress, on my right. We were five rows deep between Jaffa Gate and New Gate. The papers said there were over 25,000 people there: Israelis, Palestinians and foreigners. As we sang we released thousands of coloured balloons into the blue sky.

On the drive back through the road blocks to the West Bank and to Bethlehem I still retained in my mind's eye the colours of the mass of balloons rising in the late afternoon sun above the well proportioned rectangular walls of the Old City of Jerusalem. It occurred to me that I had not looked at the walls in that way before, or felt so moved and full of hope. May the white sweat shirts we wore, and the emblems they showed really mean "1990: Time for peace." And that reminds me I have spent the last few hours writing and my windows are as dirty as when the day began. Perhaps I will clean them tomorrow, now that the rains have gone and spring is here.

XXVIII / CHILDRENS' STREET BETHLEHEM

Childrens' Street is a long straight road which starts in front of the mosque in Assa Refugee Camp and rises, gradually at first, and then more steeply passing the theatre and sports hall complex on the western side of the Bethlehem University property. This facility, incidently, completed two years ago, has never been used by the students, since the University was closed by military order in October 1987. It is now April 1990. It is hard to believe that thirty months have passed in which we have experienced the way of life associated with the uprising.

It is on Childrens' Street, shortly after midday, that crowds of small Palestinian boys and girls make their way home from their junior school which the military recently relocated on the main Hebron Road. The Bethlehem parents complained at the arbitrary manner with which the military governor moved the primary pupils, without consultation, to what had been the secondary school premises on the hectic and very busy Hebron Road. At this new site they must cross the road to get to the school building. The traffic literally thunders down this very wide road. The secondary school pupils, by contrast, were transferred to the primary school in the safe part of town.

Two days ago I was driving the University mini bus up Childrens' Street. The way was blocked. Fifty or more five to nine year olds, including girls, were marching up the street in a wide column singing Palestinian songs, waving their small arms in the air displaying prominent "V" signs with their fingers. As they marched they covered the road with stones from the gardens and walls of the neighbouring houses. Nor did the large dust bins escape their notice. These were overturned and the refuse liberally spread across the tarmac.

You may question whether anarchy reigns. My answer would be that things are certainly not the same as they used to be. One thing is certain however; the entire student population, from five years old upwards, has been politicized by the 30 months of the Palestinian Uprising. It was more than likely that some of these young children I watched on street the other day had elder brothers who were taken by the Israeli soldiers from their classrooms a short while ago, lined up on the school play ground and systematically beaten. Such was the beating that 40 boys were sent to hospital and of these six had broken limbs.

Friends in Britain and the United States tell me they do not hear or read news about the West Bank and Gaza now. Clearly, the momentous events in other parts of the world have taken the headlines and the Intifada, the Palestinian uprising protesting 23 years of unlawful and unjust military occupation by Israel has receded into the background. Furthermore, the Israeli authorities are accomplishing what Doctor Kissinger advised two years ago when the uprising was identified, "seal it and crush it." Censorship is now far tighter. The Israeli army saturates the West Bank and Gaza with its presence.

Army tactics have been adapted and have become more effective. I counted seven roof top control and observation posts with heavily armed troops on a two mile stretch of the Hebron Road between Bethlehem and Soloman's Pools the other day. Three of us were travelling to the village of Beit Umma where the young cousin of one of our graduates was shot in the back of the head and killed recently. The young fourteen year old boy was standing, quite innocently with his two uncles on the hillside near his house, when a soldier shot him with a dumdum bullet from a house top a quarter of a mile away. His skull was shattered like an egg shell.

We were attempting to express our sympathies with the family but were prevented from doing so because the village was sealed off. We tried to send messages into the village in the hope that the graduate could sneak across the vineyard slopes from his house on the hill for we had moved down the Hebron road and could be seen from his house. We were only on the road a few minutes when officers in a jeep drew up. Obviously they were called in by the troops from the road block. Identity cards or passports were curtly demanded.

We discovered shortly afterwards that no one could move from the houses, large sections of the village were under curfew. At the same time we were surprised to see a large Palestinian flag hanging prominently over the valley slopes near the village. The Israeli army generally takes measures to see these national emblems are removed as soon as possible. The flag was attached to the wires of electricity cables thirty to forty feet above the ground. It was a sign of hope for us. Three weeks later we passed Beit Umma on our way to Hebron. To our surprise we noticed the flag was still there. Apparently the soldiers were at a loss to find a method that would remove the emblem. The villagers told us that the young people had put the flag up in a place where the ground was much closer to the wires. Evidently, and much to their delight, the wind blew the flag down the electric cables away from the higher slopes of the valley so that the distance between the flag and the ground doubled.

Such were our childish delights during the short time we stood by the road. However, we were soon reminded of the oppressive presence of the army. Over 20 army vehicles, mainly patrol jeeps and trucks, drove by. We were also dismayed to see the rapid growth and extent of the new Jewish settlements covering the neighbouring hills.

I think I can understand why the five, six and seven year olds chant Palestinian songs up Childrens' Street. Every family in the land is acutely aware of the oppression and who are the oppressors. Since the Intifada began at least 825 Palestinians have died. 80,000 have been wounded and 60,000 have suffered various forms of imprisonment, as a result of Israeli army action or settlers' activities.

What does this mean to the British reader? Let me play the numbers game though I am as aware as anybody that mere numbers and statistics can be of limited value. The Palestinian population of 1.5 million stands in ratio to that of United Kingdom at approximately 1 to 37. The 825 Palestinians gunned down, 80,000 wounded and the 60,000 imprisoned by Israeli soldiers and settlers, would compare with 30,525 deaths in United Kingdom 2,960,000 injured and 2,220,000 imprisoned. If the population of the United States is considered then the ratio is as great as 1 to 160. The total figures would be appalling with 132,000 killed, 12,800,000 injured and 9,600,000 imprisoned.

But such raw comparisons need refining. When I visited the rehabilitation centre for the Intifada wounded in Bethlehem two days ago I saw a young 23 year old mother, helpless in a wheel chair. She had been shot in the back of the head and now looked like a withered old woman. She would be a quadraplegic for life. The impact of this tragedy appalled me in all its human sadness and injustice.

This sadness envelops the lives of all the people in the occupied territories. When the young boys and girls dispersed after their demonstration on Childrens' Street there would be little to rejoice about once they reached their homes. The West Bank economy is now virtually in ruins. Families are struggling and some find it difficult to buy food for their children. Over 100,000 people are out of work. The frequent general strikes, the curfews, particularly on the refugee camps, the almost daily road blocks, all of these impede the necessary freedom of movement which are needed for commercial life to survive.

It is of value to remind my American friends that it was the Boston Tea Party that began the revolt by the American people against an unfair and unrepresentative taxation system imposed on them by a conquering power. Here, where people have no representative government and where 1300 military orders control every aspect of life, the Israeli military government is deliberately crushing the people with oppressive taxation. Tax raids are a common occurrence. The Christian village of Beit Sahour may never fully · recover economically from the months of plunder and confiscation of goods and property savagely carried out by the army. In a wider context the imposition of the Israeli VAT on all Palestinians is blatantly illegal and contrary to the principles of the Hague Convention. New taxes are suddenly concocted and applied indiscriminately. Just recently a new car tax was served upon the population. A Palestinian university colleague explained what this meant for her. A year ago her car licence cost 350 shekels (approximately $175). Then shortly after this a new tax was imposed called "The stone throwing tax" which for her car amounted to 1550 shekels ($775), five times the car licence fee. Then last week another tax entitled, "The Molotov Cocktail Tax," consisting of 1750 shekels ($875), finally forced her to sell her car; she needs flexible transportation to do her work where she is involved in an outreach programme on the West Bank in nursery education. Sudden road blocks are frequently set up to catch those who have not paid their taxes: fines, arrest and confiscation result.

I suspect that the uprising of the Palestinians is now entering a new phase. Changes in Eastern Europe and particularly in Russia, resulting in the daily flow of Russian Jews entering Israel will have a profound effect on the situation here. The Easter celebrations of the Christians in the Old City were marred by 150 settlers occupying a large building in the Christian quarter of the Old City. The discovery that the illegal occupation of the premises was accomplished by dishonest subleasing and financed by the Israeli government with American money under the name of a Panamanian Company ignited a wave of protest. Although the Israeli Supreme High Court has ordered the settlers out, it remains to be seen whether the property will be returned to its rightful owners.

The seizure of property in the Old City is a specific example of what has gone on and is and will be accomplished by the Israeli government in the 28 square miles of annexed East Jerusalem, the whole of the West Bank and Gaza Strip. Already over 50% of the land on the West Bank and over 30% in Gaza is illegally confiscated and the Arab land comprising East Jerusalem completely annexed. Furthermore, 80% of the annual water reserves of the West Bank are diverted, either to settlers on land taken from the Palestinians or to the Israeli populations within Israel itself. At the time of writing new settlements are being established and existing ones enlarged. The American government condemns this but takes no action and at the same time promises another $400 million to finance house building for the immigrants. Inevitably, the arrival of 100,000's of Russian Jews will put further strains on the limited supplies of water and other natural resources. The Palestinians will pay the price.

It was during Easter Week that I climbed the tower of the mosque that stands on a hill to the north west of Jerusalem. It is called the Mount of Joy. It is where the crusaders caught their first sight of the Holy City; it is also the place where some historians say Samuel was buried. Today the panorama is still magnificent. In the clear spring day under a cloudless sky I could identify the sweep of the Nablus Road north to Ramallah and the Palestinian villages blending with the centuries in the rolling limestone and chalk landscape, the grey chaos the refugee camp at Kalandia and nearer Jerusalem the suburbia of Beit Hanina. Then more recent structures patterned together in modern town planning style. The massive new estates of Israeli building eating up the Arab land in annexed East Jerusalem and the new red roofed fortress settlements encircling the city some of which were on the West Bank.

Paradoxically it was on the Mount of Joy that I felt most sad. Had high summer hopes of a peace initiative been dashed again by the fears, intransigence, and democratic turmoil of the Israeli governance? It came as no surprise that the Israeli President Herzog castigated the political parties for their lack of principles and over half a million Israelis signed a petition demanding electoral reform. Were we now to steel ourselves for the even harsher injustice of a Likud minority? Was the United States administration so reliant on the approval of Jewish pressure groups that it could not act in accordance with basic human justice? Spread out before me on the Easter Jerusalem landscape was the spacial expression of their policies on the land and people.

In the distant haze I could just make out the environs of Bethlehem. I should have taken some solace and Christian hope. For a week later one of my Bethlehem Moslem students met me on Childrens' Street. He had been very depressed several weeks before when soldiers raided his small home in

Deheishah refugee camp and arrested two of his brothers and his nephew. Now he smiled. He said he had good news. On the feast that marked the end of the Ramadan fast, his young brothers and nephew suddenly arrived at the door way of their small cement dwelling. Unexpectedly the Israelis had released them from prison.

XXIX / THIRTY TWO MONTHS ON

Perhaps it was not the appropriate time to ask him three weeks after his cousin had been shot dead by an Israeli soldier. We asked all the same. We were anxious to know what the Palestinians felt after nearly 32 months of intense suffering and continuous oppression during the Intifada. He was, after all, one of our students, a trusted friend for over six years. He was married now and worked with his family growing grapes and fruit on the terraces of the limestone hills north of Hebron.

He looked across the valley where a large Jewish settlement of red roof houses were covering the summits of several hills. The fast growing rural suburbia encroached over the lands that had belonged to the Palestinians for centuries. Israeli commuters and Jewish settlers from Jerusalem and Tel Aviv now lived there on the West Bank opposite his village. There were many new houses under construction, perhaps these were designated for some of the huge inflow of Russian Jews. As he stared he said in quite a matter fact of manner: "There's no future, we are all going to die. We are going to stay but we are going to die." We understood.

I stood there with Brother Joe in the warm early summer sunshine looking at the already baked ground. When you love a people and have a high regard for them it was with a deep sense of distress and helplessness that we heard the words, "We are going to die." It was not a death that would come from the normal flow of things. They would die before their time, oppressed and beaten, imprisoned, occupied and garrisoned, disenfranchised, squeezed out economically, driven from their land and despised, with the nations of the world looking on with mild disapproval but not willing to act in their defence. It seemed the entrenched Israelis had no intention of returning what was taken by force and there remained in the Palestinian mind a sense of fate, of the inevitable that they must stoically face, after the early aspirations of nationhood inspired by the Intifada many months ago. They would not give up but at the same time there seemed to be no clear hope for the immediate future.

With thirty months of the uprising completed I was trying to listen to the genuine feelings of Palestinians whose judgement I respected and valued. I chatted with a Palestinian woman who was involved in the administration of a nursing school. She was 19 in 1948 and had witnessed the treatment her family received when the Stern Gang forced her mother and father and family at gun point from their lovely home near the Old City of Jerusalem. The family lost further property in 1967 after the Six Day War. "You know," she said, when I asked what was the difference with her experience with the Intifada in June 1990 compared with 1948 and 1967, "It's the same, it's the same." She was close to tears. "They are forcing us out bit by bit. Soon we will be put in buses and sent over the river into Jordan. It is not just, it is not fair. And then they, the Israelis, tell the world their story and the world believes them. What should we do, what to do!"

Younger voices I listen to only know the experience of the Intifada. Frequently I meet young men whom I knew as students on the campus in 1987. Every week I see them near the University attempting to continue their courses that were interrupted over two years ago. "Where have you been all this time? I haven't seen you!" I ask. They smile and most reply that they have been in prison. George, from Beit Sahour, remained in Ansar 3 for a year and then was arrested again for another 6 months. He has started studying physics again in the off campus programme. Jehad, from Deheishah, has been in prison three times as has Assad who was anxious to obtain the advice of a member of staff on his seminar otherwise he would not be able to finish it quickly and obtain his degree. He fears he could be arrested again at any time. These young men look older. What boyhood or youthful looks they had when I knew them on the campus have gone. I detect a certain hardness in them. Maher from Jericho, bright and articulate, tells me that in the "University of the Desert" (the prisons in the desert became serious places of instruction) they studied politics and followed lessons. There seemed to be a strength and stoicism in his manner and attitude that I had not noticed before. They all realized the seriousness of the situation and did not have any ready answers though they nevertheless appeared to be determined to struggle on.

I ask younger Palestinian children how they felt after so many months of the uprising. They wrote their spontaneous thoughts in English. One, a boy of 11 years, who had just had friends arrested wrote: "We are the people who want to live in peace. We are proud of the Intifada because we have brought the land to the attention of the whole world." An older girl, who is a serious student and 16 years of age, described how the Intifada changed her dreams and thoughts, that "even I have changed, I'm not the old me anymore." Another simply wrote: "I'm frustrated, angry, tired and uncomfortable. I represent nobody, even myself. I have a little hope that one day the Palestinians will be free." And another: "Why can't I be free? Why can't I live in peace? What crime did I make? Is it because I am a Palestinian?" There was that inevitable human longing: "I wish I could be like all other girls in any country. When I walk in the street I don't feel safe and so I'm always at home. I want my land and my rights back. I want to be educated. I want to be treated like a human being."

There were stronger feelings. From a young boy: "I hate the Israeli government, I hate the Israeli soldiers, I hate what they are doing to us, their way of treating us." Many felt: "terrible and miserable," "I cannot stand being alive with this situation, there should be a solution." "I am like a bird in a cage, I can't do what I like freely, I can't go out whenever I want." Many realized acutely the loss of educational opportunities that they would never attain their ambitions because "we are not making progress at school and we are two years behind" or "I want to go to university but I can't because they are closed." In all the notes there was a cry for peace and normality, a fear of "living in terror," a desire to be free and a political awareness that I had not found so strong before the Intifada.

A Palestinian professional, a doctor, told me he could survive with his family the stresses and hardships of the Intifada for another 15 months. That was a year ago. As I look back I am amazed the Palestinian people have managed to survive the onslaught aimed at every level of their lives. There came the realization that the intensity of the uprising could not be sustained continuously. The level of activity has fluctuated. Academics are busily plotting graphs demonstrating the peaks and valleys of violence and protest. And just as the graphs of the killed, wounded, imprisoned and deported seems to plateau out, with periods of quieter activity the unpredictable occurs. Recently, the murder of several Gazan Palestinians by what the papers report was a deranged Israeli, and the subsequent imposition of curfews and the resulting massive protests, particularly in Gaza, sent the casualty graphs to new peaks. The UNWRA hospitals in Gaza were reporting over 1,000 injuries and over 30 killed in several days.

Again, academics and journalists after 32 months, sense some sort of focus, phases of activity, in the events that started on the 9th of December 1987 in Gaza. Perhaps the role of the academics and reporters is to analyse the situation. I still find it hard to make firm judgements. There are, for example, even amongst the so called experts, wide differences of opinion about the causes of the Intifada, who were the initial leaders, who are the present leaders and what will happen next in the uprising. It requires great gifts of insight to look at the chaotic events that surround one day by day and see clearly the signs of the times.

Perhaps, looking back at the spontaneous and often unforeseen activities certain patterns do emerge. The mass protests that spread out of Gaza in December 1987, then to Nablus, where the people took to the streets, then on the 13th of December in East Jerusalem and eventually to the whole of the West Bank can be recognised as the opening phase. This lasted for several weeks. During this period the Israelis showed through their responses that they had been taken by surprise. Although their reaction was one of severe repression it took them some time to understand what was happening. It was also in these first weeks that the media reports shocked the international community into recognising the real state of affairs in the Occupied Territories. Condemnation of the measures taken by the Israeli army and the 21 years of occupation was widespread.

The second phase can also be fairly clearly identified. It began after the first few weeks of the uprising and lasted up until the end of 1988. Although violence continued there were new developments started by the Palestinians, new responses by the Israelis and by the international community. The Palestinians organised and consolidated. This period saw the development of organized committees and popular structures in all the towns, villages and neighbourhoods of the Occupied Territories. In some cases these committees already existed but were now brought into full action with the uprising. Associated with these structures were the mass resignations of civil employees, the organising of commercial strikes, the circulation of leaflets, the home grown economy, the tax revolt and the boycott of Israeli produce.

To counteract the growing organization of the Intifada the Israelis became more subtle in their tactics. Their response began to be directed at many different levels of the Palestinian population. The Israeli Military Government attempted to gain control with curfews, wholesale arrests without trial, imprisonment, demolition of houses, tax collection campaigns, financial, communication and travel restrictions, and sanctions against Palestinian agriculture. It was also at this time that the diplomatic stances were reformulated with the cutting of Jordanian ties with the West Bank, the Arab Summit and the formulation of the American Schultz plan.

The third phase of the uprising extended throughout 1989. In their diplomatic campaign the Palestinians sought to promote their new peace plan in order to make political gains in the international arena and to attempt to start talks for a solution with the Israelis. The Israelis did make a response to these plans, but it quickly became apparent that they were merely playing for time. In the international diplomatic arena negotiations and plans were formulated.

Where are we now as we approach the end of 1990? I do not attempt to be a political pundit or in any way an expert on international affairs in the Middle East. As I write this we are still feeling the effects of the thawing in East-West relations, and of the democratization of Eastern Europe. Suddenly it seems that the world has woken up to the advantages of democracy and enlighted capitalism. The few last outposts of old-fashioned communism are beginning to look as anachronistic and strange as dinosaurs would be if they suddenly turned up in Piccadilly.

Yet at this very time of increasing hope and optimism for the world as a whole the situation in the Middle-East has never looked more grave. Even before Iraq's invasion of Kuwait there was an increasing mood of pessimism amongst the Palestinians with whom I spoke.

Though many young Palestinians are determined to stay some student friends of mine who have graduated, been in prison and who have lived in the highly politically motivated atmosphere of the refugee camps are leaving the country. They are saddened but they see little future for them in the land of their fathers. They have already sacrificed much and now want to get on with their lives having lost so many years already. Can they be blamed for thinking this way? What do you say to a young woman graduate who spent six years getting her degree under very difficult circumstances and who now sits imprisoned at home for weeks on end in utter despair unable to find a job? She is one of 12,000 unemployed graduates. In all 100,000 Palestinians are without work.

A friend of mine who has read these additional pages to this book said that he detected a change in my attitude to the people and events that I have described. He detected a note of bitterness in the words I used. If I have changed I was not conscious of deliberately doing so. In fact when I began to write my only hope was that I would touch the hearts of all my readers and that they would come to understand the realities of life for the Palestinians in the Occupied Territories. Perhaps I have been made bitter by seeing the frustrations and sufferings of the Palestinians. The opportunity for peace has all too often faded away. I also have come to know and respect the many Israelis who have the courage to speak out when the majority of their people are still beset with fear and mistrust or are determined that a greater Israel is the only solution. I once said to one of my Israeli friends: "What can we do that will convince the Israelis that we really love them?". In the end both the Israelis and the Palestinians will have to find an answer to that question. There will be and can be no peace without compromise. It is impossible to envisage a settlement of the situation in Israel and the Occupied Territories in which one or other party will gain all their demands.

And so as we slip into Autumn a new terror has emerged to haunt the Middle East. The spectre of a cataclysmic war over the Iraqi occupation of Kuwait colours all our days. The president of the Egyptian Republic spoke early on in the conflict about how he saw events unfolding if Iraq did not withdraw. His words made me shudder, but I cannot say in all honesty that I disagreed with them. If war does come (and by the time you read these words it may have come) it will I believe turn out to be the bloodiest war since the Second World War. Whatever happens in the Gulf one fact has become abundantly clear since the invasion of Kuwait. The crisis has made it far less likely that there will be a settlement of Palestinian demands in the Occupied Territories.

EPILOGUE

Imagine: that's all it said. Bold black graffiti plastered across the grey walls of a small concrete building. Was it an electricity transformer, perhaps a pumping station, or merely another derelict building on which the message was painted? We glanced at the sign as we travelled at speed along the tree lined road, the coastal road from Ashquelon to the Gaza. We were teaching staff from Bethlehem University on our way to meet students of ours in the refugee camps in the hell hole called "The Gaza Strip."

"Imagine!" somebody remarked in the mini-bus. "It's the title of John Lennon's song," another exclaimed. After all, I mused to myself, the one who recognized the name should know, he had followed the story of the Beatles from the beginning when he started his teaching career in Liverpool in the early 1960's. Soft strolling rhythms, someone humming, someone else whistling, the melody recaptured the lyric:

"Imagine there's no heaven
She says you'll try
No hell below us
Above only the sky."

Our singing voices faded away as the van arrived at the wide check- point, the only entrance into the Gaza Strip from the north. The grey flat landscape subdued our spirits. In the dust and heat we approached the concrete and steel barriers manned by heavily armed Israeli soldiers. Raw red and white military notices, menacing watch towers armed with machine guns, ugly prefabricated huts, coils of barbed wire and high steel fences marked the entrance to the biggest human prison I know. Apprehension and fear descended on our motley party as we showed our passports to puzzled soldiers who registered surprise on their faces. I could see them wondering why it was that these British and American teachers should wish to come to this place only days after the 24-hour curfews imposed during the Gulf War on the West Bank and Gaza, had ended. The reason which I could have told them if they had asked, was provided by the three dusty cars with Gaza number plates waiting for us on the other side of the ugly barriers. I wish the Israeli soldiers could have seen the greeting we received from the group of young and mature students from Gaza. This Easter Monday, 1991, was the first time I had seen them since the fall semester at Bethlehem University that ended at Christmas 1990. How could they still smile having endured one of the most savage and inhuman consecutive 40 day 24-hour curfews in the confines of their concrete huts in the refugee camps? Prisons within a prison.

"Imagine there's no country
It isn't hard to do
Nothing to kill or die for
And no religion too."

That Monday, they drove us to their homes and through the obscene grey chaos of the camps: Jabalia in the North, Bureij, Nuseirat, Maghazi and Beach Camp in the centre of the strip; Beach Camp was on the coast adjoining Gaza city. We did not have time to hurry through the dusty shanty turmoil of Khan Yunis and Rafah in the south of the strip. The notion that there are nearly 700,000 Palestinians, 370,000 of them refugees in cramped camps in an area 40 km long and 12 km wide is hard to visualize. To picture a people living in what must be one of the highest population densities in the world of 1730 per square km, is difficult to comprehend. Here 60% of the population are under 19 years of age, and 77% under 29 years of age. There is also a birthrate in Gaza of 45 per 1000, again one of the highest in the world.

Consider, too, that nearly 40% of the limited land space has been confiscated for approximately 3000 Jewish settlers who utilize the best physical resources in the area at the expense of the indigenous population. For example, the average Gazan receives only 1% of the water a Jewish settler consumes, in a situation where the use of water exceeds natural replenishment: the drop in the water table causes increasing salinization of wells available to Gazans. And then perhaps ponder that these people are imprisoned and ghettoised within this small impoverished area for over 40 years and have suffered military occupation for 24 years. Reflect also that during and since the Gulf War this enslavement has intensified. How was it that one of our number kept singing the tune?

"Imagine all the people
Living life in peace.
You say I'm a dreamer
But I'm not the only one,
I'll hope some day you'll join us
And the world will be one."

Under laden lemon and orange trees in an orchard near Bureij camp one of the mature student teachers invited us to eat lunch. Earlier we had insisted that there should be no meal since the Muslims were fasting during Ramadan and families hardly had food enough to feed their own. We could not persuade our Muslim friends, so we were made to sit and recline on mats, blankets and cushions placed on the grass in the shade of the orchard. Arabic salads, rice and chicken "Macklubeh," called "Upside Down" in English, was served with the generosity so typical of Arab households. Our student and teacher college friends sat with us but did not break their fast and such was their courtesy and graciousness that our embarrassment rapidly subsided. As we broke bread in their presence I could not help feel we experienced in some strange way an Easter celebration with Christian and Muslims together.

"Imagine no possessions,
I wonder if you can,
No need for grief or hunger
A brotherhood of man."

Two weeks later after our visit to Gaza I unexpectedly returned there. My second visit was connected to the first since one of the main reasons for the earlier visit was an attempt to help our 160 students from the strip to continue their studies. The restrictions imposed during the Gulf War made it very difficult for Gaza students to travel to Bethlehem to continue their studies so alternative ways of continuing their education were being explored. After the Gulf War, the Israeli authorities would only allow Palestinians to move from one sector to another if the individual had been issued a permit. One of our Gaza students had been caught by the Gulf War and could not leave Bethlehem because of the devastating 24-hour curfews that lasted for weeks. He desperately needed to get back to Gaza as his permit had expired and he had not seen his family for three months. He also wished to celebrate the Muslim feast at the end of Ramadan with his family.

He was fearful that if he attempted to return to the check point at the entrance to Gaza on his own he would be beaten and imprisoned. He explained to me how he was standing by his friend Isac Abu Srur and saw him shot through the head by an Israeli soldier on the university campus in October 1987. Only a few days after this tragedy he was arrested by the military and remained in prison for nearly three years. Could an expatiate escort him? Transport arrangements promised by a foreign agency did not materialize and he was stranded in Jerusalem. I took him to a student's home in the Old City of Jerusalem and then drove him down to Gaza the following day. Soldiers at the check-point inspected my British passport and my university identity card. I explained to them that the young Palestinian with me was one of my students from Bethlehem University. They were most insistent that I drive only several hundred yards to the nearest petrol station inside the strip and then return immediately; I had yellow Israeli number plate which could mean I would be attacked in Gaza.

No sooner had I driven 20 yards through the barrier than the student instructed me to turn down a rough road to the left towards his village of Beit Hanoun. In the mirror I snatched a glance at the astonished faces of the Israeli soldiers behind. The short cut to his village involved negotiating rows of concrete blocks across the uneven winding track and a rather large mound of dirt that needed climbing over. I shuddered to think what the university authorities would have said had they witnessed the hill climb. My student companion hung out of the window of the car as we approached his home village shouting in Arabic in a reassuring manner to all we met that contrary to what they saw we were in fact a friendly visitation.

Eventually the frantic driving round crowded narrow lanes and streets terminated down an untidy alley. All the extended family, 29 of them, crowded out to greet him. And then his mother arrived. She had not seen or heard from him for three months and had no idea what may have happened to him during the Gulf War. I tell you to see mother and son together again was worth a hundred risky journeys to Gaza!

The experience described in Gaza occurred 13 months after I had revised the stories in "Children of Bethlehem" in June 1990. Much has changed since then and the narrative could well be extended to include the events here in the Occupied Territories that led up to the Gulf War, the catastrophe of the war itself, and its devastating aftermath for the Palestinians. During this period the crushing impact of the Israeli Occupation intensified. When the Gulf War started in mid January Israel imposed a strict blanket 24-hour curfew for over a month on the entire Palestinian population. This initiated an entirely new phase in Israel's 24 year-long military occupation. The noose tied around the oppressed Palestinian society was drawn even tighter; the combination of land confiscations, enlargement and foundation of new settlements on Arab land, the ghettoisation and systematic destruction of the Palestinian economy has accelerated. Life is now made so hard that those Palestinians that can leave the country sadly do so; auto-transfer is a deliberate policy designed by the Israelis.

The Palestinian patrimony has been plundered whilst the world stands by doing little about it; the people are exhausted and demoralized. They sacrificed so much during the Intifada and now wonder what the suffering has achieved. The Intifada continues though it is difficult to assess what form it is now taking. The army of occupation has far greater control, the oppressed population are weary and tired of endless strikes, blanket punishments, imprisonment, the evils associated with collaborators and the overwhelming sense that life here is even more untenable than ever before. A sequel to this book would be necessary to tell the story of the past dramatic 12 months.

My conversation in the car journey 12 weeks ago with the student from Gaza brought to mind the many faces of students and friends I have become acquainted with over the last six years. What has happened to these human beings recounted in the stories in this little book? Those students I taught in my first class in October 1985 will graduate this summer; it has taken them six years. Now Bethlehem University is open again we have completed two 12 week semesters, one before the Gulf War and one after. (Though Bethlehem University has been open this academic year 1990-91, most of the other Palestinian universities remain closed and after four years of closure still await military orders to enable them to open.) Close friends like Noah will graduate and have already taken leadership roles in their damaged society. He has already been responsible for the development of a new dental clinic in Deheisheh Camp and is now actively trying to raise funds to start a childrens' library so desperately needed there. Others are now married, some with children; Saleh, like Noah, has two children. Yousif, whose house was blown up by the Israelis, raised funds and rebuilt his home on land he purchased with the help of young American students. He now works for the UN and has won a scholarship in a university peace programme in the United States.

The young man Khalid, responsible for the stories in Chapter VII, has left the country like so many other bright Palestinians. Graduate friends from the village of Beit Ummar still come to see us and it is most interesting that we now have over 60 students from this particular village present as undergraduates in the university. And Maysoon, seriously wounded by a high velocity dum dum bullet in her leg, eventually managed to receive permission to have a specialized operation in Canada. The delay prevented the surgeons from achieving a complete recovery; she will always need a brace around her leg. At present she is working hard to complete her degree and repeatedly invites me to visit her home in Bani Na'im. Khalil, Taha, Fursan the tallest freshman of the year, Magdolean the singer, Sihan and Suzan and so many others, once they graduate will find life very difficult for there are virtually no jobs to go to.

Friendship with Palestinian families continues and deepens. Claudette and Michel continued to struggle with their family of growing adults and adolescents. Close relatives of theirs lost their only son during the Gulf War. He was shot through the head by a lawless settler while talking to his mother in their kitchen one evening during the long curfew. The Jewish settler from Russia continues to drive his car past their house in Beit Sahour each evening as he returns to his expanding settlement on confiscated Arab land. He remains unpunished and free. Perhaps my conversations three months ago in the car with the student on the way to Gaza has focused these reminiscences more clearly in my mind.

Three months ago I passed through the check point from Gaza later that day to return to Bethlehem. I noticed on my return journey the black graffiti was painted on both sides of the concrete building so that drivers could see the sign when leaving Gaza:
    "Imagine all the people
    Sharing all the world

You may say I'm a dreamer
But I'm not the only one
I hope some day you will join us
And the world will live as one."

Who painted the black letters? An Israeli or a Palestinian? I wonder?
Incidentally, I have just heard on the radio as I finish writing this in late
July 1991, that Mr. Baker on leaving after his latest visit to Jerusalem
and the Middle East expressed real optimism for peace talks.
"You may say, I'm a dreamer."
Imagine.

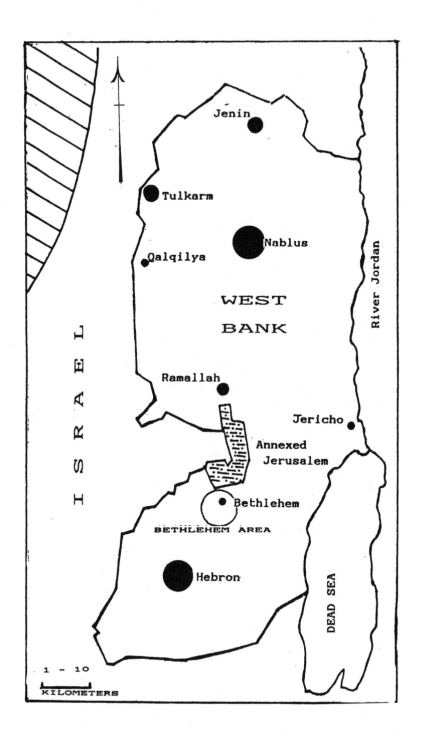

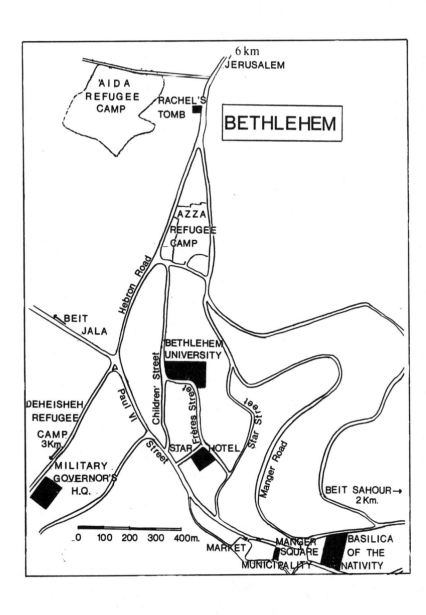

6 km
JERUSALEM

'AIDA
REFUGEE
CAMP

RACHEL'S
TOMB

BETHLEHEM

AZZA
REFUGEE
CAMP

Hebron Road

BEIT
JALA

BETHLEHEM
UNIVERSITY

Children' Street

Frères Street

Star Str.

Paul VI

DEHEISHEH
REFUGEE
CAMP
3Km.

MILITARY
GOVERNOR'S
H.Q.

Street

STAR HOTEL

Manger Road

BEIT SAHOUR→
2 Km.

_0 100 200 300 400m.

MARKET

MANGER
SQUARE

MUNICIPALITY

BASILICA
OF THE
NATIVITY

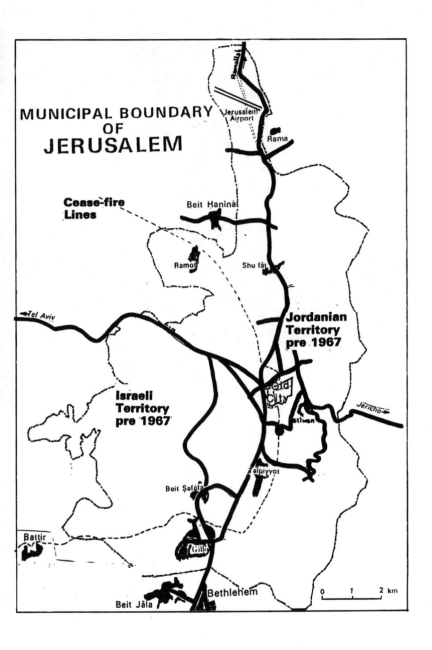

MUNICIPAL BOUNDARY
OF
JERUSALEM

Cease-fire
Lines

Jordanian
Territory
pre 1967

Israeli
Territory
pre 1967

Jerusalem
Airport

Rama

Beit Haninà

Ramot

Shu fât

Tel Aviv

Old
City

Silwan

Jericho

Talpiyyot

Beit Ṣafàfa

Battir

Gilo

Bethlehem

Beit Jāla

0   1   2 km

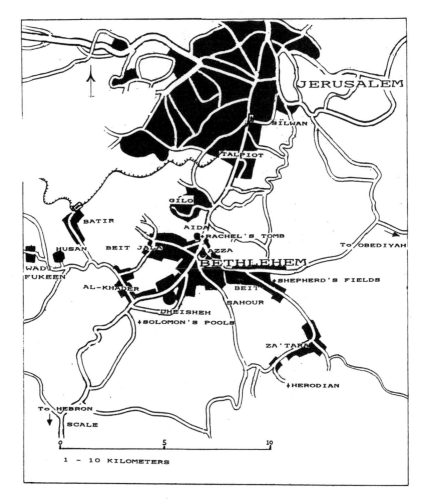

BETHLEHEM AREA

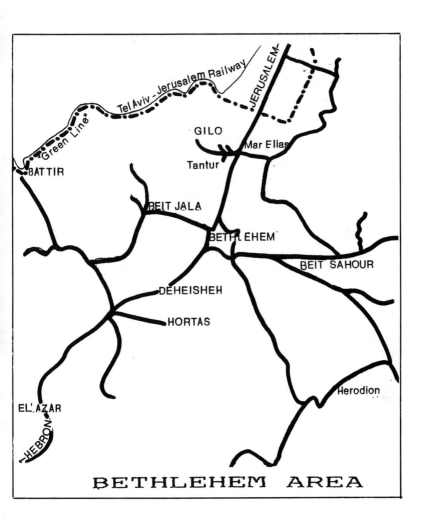

BETHLEHEM AREA

THREE YEARS OF INTIFADA AND OF

HUMAN RIGHTS VIOLATIONS SUMMARY DATA
UPRISING, YEARS 1, 2, AND 3: DECEMBER 8, 1987 THROUGH DECEMBER 8, 1990

VIOLATION	Year One Dec 9/87 to Dec 8/88	Year Two Dec 9/88 to Dec 8/89	Year Three Dec 9/89 to Dec 8/90	TOTAL UPRISING TOTAL
DEATES	380	345	167	892
Shot	283	312	147	742
Non-Bullet Cause	32	19	11	62
Tear-gas Related	65	14	9	88
SERIOUS INJURIES	46,000(est)	34,000(est)	26,000(est)	**106'000**
EXPULSIONS (EDR)	32	26	-	58
Orders	56	0	-	56
ADMINISTRATIVE DETENTION (Orders)	5,000(est)	3,500(est)	4,000(est)	**12,500**
CURFEWSU	3,338	3,054	2,284	**8,676**
West Bank	1,906	1,226	1,421	4,553
Gaza	1,432	1,828	863	4,123
TREES UPROOTED	23,440	54,258	17,067	**94,765**
DEMOLIIIONS & SEALINGS	584	621	521	**1'726**
Of Houses "for securlty reasons"				
- Demollshed	108	154	150	412
- Sealed	23	107	126	256
Of Unlicensed Buildlngs (mostly houses)				
- Demolished	425	319	241	985
IndirectDemolitlons	28	41	1	70
By Settlers	-	-	3	3
PERSONS DISPIACED	5'000+	5'500+	4'500 1	**15'000**

source: Palestine Human Rights Information Center, P.O. Box 20479, Jerusalem, Israel